pitm
2000
SHORTHAND

DICTATION PRACTICE

B W Canning

Pitman Publishing

First published 1975
Reprinted 1975

SIR ISAAC PITMAN AND SONS LTD
Pitman House, Parker Street, Kingsway, London WC2B 5PB
PO Box 46038, Banda Street, Nairobi, Kenya

PITMAN PUBLISHING PTY LTD
Pitman House, 158 Bouverie Street, Carlton, Victoria 3053, Australia

PITMAN PUBLISHING CORPORATION
6 East 43rd Street, New York, NY 10017, USA

THE COPP CLARK PUBLISHING COMPANY
517 Wellington Street West, Toronto 135, Canada

PITMAN PUBLISHING CO SA (PTY) LTD
Craighall Mews, Jan Smuts Avenue, Craighall Park,
Johannesburg 2001, South Africa

Isaac Pitman

ISBN: 0 273 00886 0

Text set in 10/11 pt Monotype Baskerville, printed by photolithography, and bound in Great Britain at The Pitman Press, Bath.
G5—(S2003:26)

PREFACE

This text, with the *Workbook* (*Parts 1* and *2*) and the pre-recorded dictation on cassette or open reel, is intended to be used alongside *First Course* which explains the theory of the system.

Dictation Practice comprises seventeen sections. Section 1 corresponds with Units 1–5 of *First Course*; Section 2 is designed for use in class as soon as Unit 6 has been completed; Section 3 after Unit 7, and so on. It also contains 26 longer dictation passages at the end of the book; 23 of these appear in shorthand in the *Workbook* for reading, copying and copied dictation practice, and the remainder are intended for "free" dictation by the teacher as required. It is recommended that students should use *Dictation Practice*. Students who are able to resolve a reading difficulty by immediate reference to the printed longhand in *Dictation Practice* will not on that account be less, but more efficient writers and readers. The vital thing is that during the learning stage, students should think all the time about the shorthand that they are copying or writing from dictation.

Each section of this book has a standard pattern: short form practice; phrases; dictation in three parts—(*a*) easy, (*b*) and (*c*) standard; theory checks and free dictation. All of these, except the theory checks and free dictation, are in shorthand in the *Workbook*.

In each section, the Theory Checks are composed of twenty words based on the theory taught to that point. As these are intended primarily as a check on students' progress, it is suggested that they be used by teachers as follows:

(*a*) Write up the words in longhand on a chalkboard and ask the students to write them in shorthand in their correct positions and with vowels inserted, allowing a two or three minute time limit.

(*b*) Write up the words in shorthand, read them to the students once, and then remove them and ask the students to write them from the book, or from the chalkboard longhand, allowing a two-minute time limit.
(*c*) Give the outlines on an unlined chalkboard and ask the students to copy them, writing them in their correct position and inserting the vowels, allowing a two-minute time limit.

The passages of free dictation, each of about 100 words, do not appear in shorthand in *Dictation Practice Workbook Parts 1* and *2*. For the most part all shorthand used in the learning stage is better prepared by the reading approach to encourage a high standard of accurate shorthand writing. However, the challenge of writing from new material is motivating and interesting, and it is worthwhile to include it in the programme from time to time. Care has been taken to ensure that most of the words used are those that the students have already seen and written before.

It is my hope that this book, the *Workbook Parts 1* and *2*, and the recorded material will prove to be of lasting value to students in helping them to become quick and efficient shorthand writers, and speedy and accurate transcribers.

B W Canning, 1975

CONTENTS

SECTION 1
UNITS 1 to 5
of Pitman 2000 First Course

1 SHORT FORM PRACTICE

(*a*) Short forms and derivatives are given in sets of twenty for dictation at the beginning of each Section.

is	of	the	today
any	thing	I	nothing
with	this	for	be
we	yesterday	has	are
yourself	manufacture	hour	thanked

it	to	manufacturer	being
you	anything	thanking	yours
have	all	do	manufacturing
but	will	and	are
yours	ours	something	with

(*b*) Short forms are included in sentences and the phrasing to be used is indicated by hyphens.

(i) Have-you any of-this in-your-case? **(8)**

(ii) I-have to-go with-you to-the boat and-I-have nothing to-take. **(15)**

(iii) Are-you going to-the manufacturers today? We-were with-them yesterday. **(12)**

(iv) I-thank-you for-the things and-I-have something for-you to-sell today. **(15)**

(v) Do-you yourself have any of-the soap manufactured for-us yesterday? **(12)**

2 PHRASES

of the, to the, and the, but the, with the, are the, do the, all the, this is, they will, to us, with us, for us, we are, and is the, they are, with you, we will be, they will be, it will be the, as we are, to go, it is, it is the, they were, and is, and as.

3 DICTATION

(a) Easy

Have you any space in your desk for the comb / and the soap? **(13)**

We are going to sell some of the red cases / today. We will have the yellow cases in for Monday. / **(20)**

It is our custom to work Sundays too, and this / is the sole way we have any success in getting / enough of our manufactures to our customers. They have road, / rail and airways to take them. **(36)**

We have saved enough of the boards, and the door / will be repaired. **(13)**

We were told the name for the cases of dates / but we have no way of getting to them though / they were stowed in the boat yesterday. **(27)**

This is a firm we know is having success in / Rome in selling cases of eggs, sets of tapes, and / loads of maize. **(23)**

Some of you will be delayed as the railway is / being repaired, but you will all be in the boat / sailing Sunday. **(22)**

Will you get some of the roses to us today? / We have to take them with us in the boat / and we will sail for Bear Lake Bay. **(28)**

I will come to your firm today for the purpose / of repairing all the desks. It may be I will / have to delay doing some of them. We have to / take care to do the work in a thorough way / and it may take some days. Some things may take / hours. **(51)**

(b) Standard

I have faith in both of them. They will do / the work with no errors and they will cope with / anything they are faced with. **(25)**

All you have to do is to go to your / manufacturers, taking with you the sets of tapes. They will / make some sets for you of any length and in / any colours. **(32)**

As space for us all becomes less, we will have / to take care of the earth. We have failed to / take enough care and things will get worse in the / months to come. Something may be saved and we will / be forced to take up less aimless ways. We have / the lesson of today with us but have we read / it, and will we have success in doing things we / know we have to do to save the earth? (**79**)

We have loaded all the cases of eggs and bales / of rope and the boat has sailed for the Cape / with them. Some things are delayed in customs and they / will go to Yale Airways and will get to the / Cape for sale to all customers Monday and Wednesday. (**49**)

We thank you for taking all those rolls of tapes / to your firm. We have saved them for you for / some months as we guessed they may be an aid / to you in the work you are doing in the / Bay Lake case. (**43**)

(c) **Standard**

Will you be taking all your eggs to the fair? / We have twelve cases in the cells below this subway / you may care to sell. Will you take them too? / We will sell them to you for a low sum / and we know you will get customers for all of / them. We will take them up the subway and load / them for you today. You will have no delay in / getting them to the fair. (**75**)

The vessel sailed for Exmouth yesterday with a load of / rails and oak doors. They were forced to go in / to the bay to take in seventy-six cases of / sago. Sums were raised for this purpose as the sago / is going as aid for the young folk. (**48**)

We swayed as the boat rose and fell in the / swell. We were forced to stow the load and we / thanked the young folk for the way they had worked / the sails to save the boat in the gale. Tell / them all to come to the Cape for some pay / as we have no way of getting it to them. / (**60**)

Stay in the boat and take in this length of / rope. The oars are below the deck boards. Take them / and row to the bay as you have to get / the case of maize Beth has for you. You will / have enough space to stow it. In the bay go / to the Yellow Bird pub and tell them you have / the case in the boat. They will come with you / to get it, and pay you the sum our customers / have said they will pay with something for you, too. / (**90**)

4 THEORY CHECKS

spaces	named	phases	senseless
date	coal	mailed	yellow
making	unsafe	error	coloured
spade	vague	desks	airways
soaks	wedding	Monday	forces

5 FREE DICTATION

Our sales this month rose, but we are getting some / customers failing to pay sums to us in Lake Bay. / Our sales of coal are up as are the sales / of gates and oak doors. In the months to come / we will aim to raise our work force and to / do all thorough repairs the firm has failed to do / to date. We thank both rail and airways for the / aid in getting manufactures to our customers. Our Board will / take care it gets all the work of the firm / going in making the things for sale in vogue today. / We will make this our aim, but we may make / some errors. **(112)**

SECTION 2

UNIT 6

of Pitman 2000 First Course

1 SHORT FORM PRACTICE

(*a*)

has	could	manufacturing	manufactured
will	thank	have	your
thanked	would	to	yesterday
the	this	with	that
any	it	you	in
thank	could	as	of
and	thing	but	is
would	your	we	our
it	be	manufactures	I
his	thanks	yours	nothing

(*b*)

(i) Could-you let-us-know your suede coat manufactures for-this month? **(12)**

(ii) You failed to-tell-us the things that are manufactured in-this port. **(13)**

(iii) The things you spoke of yesterday are being sent to-the port today. **(13)**

(iv) They would-have come to-the game but they-have to-stay in-the port to-thank-the manufacturer. **(19)**

(v) We-could go to-the lake for-you. We-will let-you-know today. **(14)**

2 PHRASES

I will let you know, we were, they were, in the, would you, would you be, it will be, it would be, would it, with us, to us, for us, that it is, that it would be, that we were, will you, I will, I may, I came, this is, that is the, it is said.

3 DICTATION

(a) Easy

We waited for the coats, but they came too late / with the result that the boat sailed and the coats / were left in the port. (**25**)

You may know we wrote and said that the weight / of the coats you manufactured for us is too low. / We will take them to sell as some of our / export work. Could you make up some of the coats / for us of a weight selected for our sales? Let / us have a note of the rates you will expect / to manufacture them for us. (**65**)

We will be selecting some of the cases of soap / you sent us and we expect to sell them in / a month. We will deduct the sum we spoke of / and, except for this, we will pay all the debt / as you said in your note to us. We have / raised our export sales and we will aim for some / success in the months to come. (**66**)

The port is located in the bay and we expect / you to raise its export sales in the months to / come. Support for this comes in the report that Ray / Bell wrote for the Port Board, and in this it / is said that the manufacturers will come to the port. / They all have faith in the manufacturers and the work / force and expect exports in manufactured things and in maize, / nuts and potatoes. (**73**)

(b) Standard

Some of our customers sailed in the vessel and they / have left some things in it. Would you go to / get them for us? Some have left cases, photos and / things. You could go the Lake Road way and take / the railway to Exmouth and save some hours. We will / pay all your fares and any sums expected—customs and / port rates. We have to stay with them in the / port and may be delayed. Will you support us in / this way? (**82**)

I spoke to the lake folk in the pub yesterday. / They said they have swum the lake and swept it / with nets but they have yet to locate the eighteen / cases of gold sunk in the boat 'Belle of Exmouth'. / They swear the swell in the lake is getting up / and it is unsafe for our methods yet. It is / up to us to take some of them with us. / We will wait some days and board in the pub. / We will aim to get that gold though we may / be delayed. (**92**)

Take a bucket and spade and get some bait. We / will have to sweat to get it but it will / be well worth it. I will work in the meadow, / remote though it is, and you may go to the / bay in the boat. I expect you will get some. / I know that it will be kept wet. (**58**)

(c) **Standard**

Sirs, We wrote yesterday to tell you that you have / yet to pay for the fourteen cases of nuts we / sent you in May. You have paid for the cases / of maize but the debt for the nuts is yet / unpaid. Will you pay today? That being the case we / could let you have the bonus we spoke of. Any / delay in paying all the debt this month will result / in our cutting the bonus. We will be forced to / do this, as we have to report to our Board. / Deduct the bonus and pay today. This is the fair / thing to do. (**103**)

We will sell suede coats in red, yellow and slate / colours for export. The cut and the care we take / in the manufacture of our coats will sell them for / us. Our work is thorough and we repair all coats / for eighteen months. We have all faith in the worth / of the coats and we have left some with you. / Will you let us know, supposing it is your purpose, / to take some of them for your customers? Make a / note of the rates we let sellers of our manufactures / have. Sales of eighty-five and up will get you / our bonus rates—something for all our customers to aim / for! (**111**)

4 THEORY CHECKS

kept	skate	evades	swearing
net	codes	meadow	swelled
effects	lessons	mate	spokes
supported	locating	lotus	waited
saints	deducted	potatoes	yet

5 FREE DICTATION

The effects of the net sales to all the customers / located in this port were debated yesterday. Some said that / the results were those expected; some said that the raised / sales would force the roads and railways to make repairs / and pay sums that they would have no success in / raising. They would have to have aid, else they could / well fail. Would a debate be enough? We have to / make a thorough report, they said, taking note of all / the effects of the sales, and of our care for / the Lake folk, too. They have to know that, except / for us, things could be worse for them. (**108**)

SECTION 3
UNIT 7
of Pitman 2000 First Course

1 SHORT FORM PRACTICE

(*a*)

his	shall	all	had
in	would	thanking	anything
something	which	do	large
that	for	today	being
will	on	manufacture	dollar
with	on	this	could
shall	to	dollar	have
and	had	thanks	thing
which	for	has	think
nothing	have	yesterday	large

(*b*)

(i) We-shall all get something for-the work we-do. **(10)**
(ii) I-shall get a large sum today in dollars. **(9)**
(iii) I-had large sales in May and I-expected them. **(10)**
(iv) The dollars which-we-sent-you, I-had to-get in Essex. **(12)**
(v) On-the-way to-the lake yesterday we-were on-the road for two hours. **(15)**

2 PHRASES

I shall, I shall be, we shall have, which is, in which the, which are, which were, which we have, is the, on the, on the way, and is the, I had, I had the, we had the, as it, as it is, as it is the, as we are, as we were.

3 DICTATION

(a) Easy

We note that you are waiting for a large sum / which is on its way to you today. Will you / let us have your cheque for the sum you have / to pay? We shall be expecting it on Wednesday. Thank / you. **(41)**

The effect of the words on page 16 of the / budget for your estate, which came to us yesterday, is / that the sums you will have to pay in rates / will be less. We showed the budget to Joe Dale / and Joe thinks that some changes should be effected in / the methods of paying on page 14. I have sent / you a note on this. **(65)**

We are all expecting that the changes it is our / purpose to make in your manufacturing methods will have the / effect of raising your sales. We shall show you the / way to get the customers for your beds and bedding / and to raise your export sales too. Much of the / work for this is shaping well. Yet with some rush / we shall have the report for you on the fourth / of May. **(72)**

We have read the pages which you have selected for / us, and we support all you say in your report. / The budget is fair and it shows that the exchange / rate will be of some aid to the changes which / it is the purpose of the Board to make. **(49)**

(b) Standard

We have raised the wages of our work force, but / we shall be getting raised manufactures too, so our customers / will go on paying the same. The result will be / large sales in such exports as gates and doors, benches / and desks. We expect all our customers will go on / supporting us. Changes, in the shape of export and exchange / rates, will be for us. **(65)**

Our Dutch customers will be coming to lunch on Monday. / They are coming in a jumbo jet and will be / met in the airport. We shall take them to the / Red Range and as they are coming for the Egg / Month they expect us to have poached eggs and such / things in which eggs come into the making. So you / may take the estate to the airport to fetch them / to the Red Range. They say they have chosen to / stay with us for the month so it is up / to us to do all the expected things for them. /(**100**)

The Judge on this bench is aged seventy-two, is / sage, and his errors are rare. The Judge is an / expert on chess and this has kept the young touch / to his work which we noted in our 'Page for / Today' in 'The Mail'. (**44**)

(c) Standard

They say that we will get large shells on the / edge of the lake which has shoals of tench too. / Will you check this for us? We could escape the / dull work of the firm for a month with a / boat on the lake. Those young enough may take buckets / and spades. The old will stay on the shore in / the sun and air. (**64**)

Shall we get James Wade to judge the bulbs in / the show which is on a Sunday in May? Is / it the fourth? James has the touch for the folk / we get in the show, and has an expert's eye / for all shades of colour and shape. The Dutch respect / his thoroughness and have sent for James to come to / judge for them in a month, maybe two. James works / on the estate of Sir Bert Rhodes and I expect / we could get a 'yes' but we would have to / get in touch and this is the way you could / aid us. Will you do it? (**106**)

The edge of this page is cut and has a / shade of red but those pages are all yellow. It / is for us to take on the expert work of / making a report on this. Such pages are rare. We / have to judge with care and make no errors, for / we shall be slated for them. (**56**)

May we take it you will do some of the / work for us? We have read the essay you wrote / on this and as we know your work well, we / suppose you will be getting it to us on Monday. / We shall take on the work of checking any pages / left untouched for the report we have to make on / Thursday. (**61**)

4 THEORY CHECKS

weight	edgeways	pages	chosen
code	shaping	bases	wages
met	essays	bunch	ledge
meadow	escaped	shed	remote
cheque	touch	choke	left

5 FREE DICTATION

Some of the firm's customers are having to pay large / sums in wages. Sales of manufactures are low, so they / evade paying debts for months. The result is that we / fail to get the dollars and we delay paying our / debts too. We shall have to tell the Board of / this and say to them that the repairs will have / to wait. In May, a sale of our coats is / expected to raise the level of exports and a change / will come. Our guess is that we shall be manufacturing / coats on a large scale for exporting to our customers / in twelve months, maybe less. (**105**)

SECTION 4
UNIT 8
of Pitman 2000 First Course

1 SHORT FORM PRACTICE

(*a*)

ought	also	any	but
always	owe	something	we
on	manufacturer	owes	hour
is	your	all	owing
are	it	thanking	of
owe	ought	owing	with
do	owes	yourself	large
today	the	manufactured	owed
to	shall	in	always
also	is	have	although

(*b*)

(i) They-will-be coming to-the market for an hour today. (**11**)
(ii) Owing to-our losses we ought not to-manufacture for-this market also. (**13**)
(iii) Anything you say will always-be reported in 'The Mail'. (**10**)
(iv) The fact is that-they also owe-us a large sum in cash. (**13**)
(v) Some of-them always come but-they-are away owing to-lack of cash. (**14**)

2 PHRASES

we were, we are, in which, on the, would you, will you, they were, I will, I may, I came, with the, with us, with them, this charge, your charges, bank charges, manufacturing charge, top form, bank forms, your forms, it was, it was not.

3 DICTATION

(a) Easy

We are going shopping in the car and we shall / all depart sharp at two. Take care to have enough / cash with you to get your things as the bank / will be shut. In the market I saw some job / lots which we ought to get. Some of them we / shall have to repair and make up well for sale / to our customers. I suppose we could make a large / sum in this way. We will have to take large / bags for the things bought and we will work on / them tomorrow to adapt them for selling in our shop. / **(100)**

Although the road passes the farm it is a long /way away. You could depart at two and get to / it in two hours. As it is your purpose to / set off tomorrow you will have to get a large / sum of cash at the bank today. Ask them for / a bank form and take it to the farmer. We / shall have to pay customs charges as we are going / to export the maize, and the farmer will have to / mark the form for us so that we may get / back some of the cash. The maize will be packed / in large sacks and you may have to weigh them / on the spot, as we have to know the weight / both for customs and for loading on the boat. **(129)**

(b) Standard

Our lawyers say that this is a bad act and / it may well do us some damage in the export / market. We shall have to manage in some way to / bar it getting adopted and this is a job for / today, not tomorrow. Your part is to watch the way / things go, as I shall have to go to York / today to tell our customers all we are doing to / bar it. They may well have some facts that will / aid us in the attack on this law. I shall / tell them we are working to get a fair result. / **(100)**

The map tells us that we have to follow this / path to get to Red Rock. The path is bad / and goes up the face of the rock, so we / have to take care. Take ropes with you and watch / yourselves or you may fall. At the top of Red / Rock is a small cottage. It was in the cottage / some months ago that we caught a large, yellow-spotted / moth called a

Yellow Shadow and rare in this part. / Maybe we shall have the same luck. Have you all / got your packets of egg and tomato rolls and your / cups too? On the way back we will call at / the Bell Cafe so do have them with you. Well, / let us set off. Take care nothing is left as / we go. **(132)**

(c) Standard

Things have changed so much that all our shops report / large losses. This is because today they are not located / for the market. We met to talk of this two / months ago but though it was debated for hours, it / all came to nothing. Our losses go on in the / same way and the banks will not support us long, / as I expect you know. We have to cut our / losses, raise large sums of cash and get shops located / in those parts we know will do well. I am / willing to bet all I have that they will be / a success. We have to do this or we all / fail. Pause too long and it will be too late. / **(120)**

It is not our job to sell the watches, but / we will sell them at the fair tomorrow for such / an old customer. May we ask you to tell us / the sums asked for the watches as we will have / to sell at some loss or customers may not purchase / them. We ought to get enough cash to pay in / to the bank in Low Market Road, and in this / way we think our customer may not get in debt. / **(80)**

4 THEORY CHECKS

taxes	Cork	baggage	pod
farm	tomato	walk	guard
moss	raw	attaching	facts
chopped	shocking	palms	selecting
calling	assault	regard	farmyard

5 FREE DICTATION

It is a fact that having sold so large a / part of our manufactures to this customer, we have come / to have no regard for his firm which owes us / large sums and has debts in this part of the / world, too, because of his bad luck with his export / sales to Morocco. The firm has not sent us any / cash or cheques for fifteen months. In fairness to those / sharing with us in the work we do and to / the Board which expects us to act for them, we / will have to call in the aid of the law. / **(100)**

SECTION 5
UNIT 9
of Pitman 2000 First Course

1 SHORT FORM PRACTICE

(*a*)

ought	owes	owing	thing
it	who	do	something
owe	always	you	being
is	owed	any	could
to	I	that	able to
his	owe	thank	nothing
largely	always	owes	as
able to	ought	an	but
are	also	thing	anything
owing	owed	who	will

(*b*)

(i) Who-will pay-us-the sum owed for-the glass? **(10)**
(ii) The things we make are largely manufactured in-this-port. **(10)**
(iii) Some who-will come today were unable-to come yesterday. **(10)**
(iv) Will-you be-able-to pay-the debt owing to-your customers to-day? **(13)**
(v) They-will-be-able-to pay largely in cash for anything they owe-us. **(14)**

2 PHRASES

who is, who is the, who are, who are the, who will, who will be, unable to, we are unable to, we were, it was, it was not, local charges, claim forms, is the, has the, for us, to us, with us.

3 DICTATION

(a) Easy

The Black Rose Cafe is the place chosen for the / lunch today and I may get to it but it / will be touch and go. Jack Clay will be paying / for it as the lunch is largely for his customers. / The Cafe has a cup and two medals for the / old glass and gold plate they show and for the / large oak tables and settles which are dated 1562./ **(71)**

Sir, We enclose a cheque for $37 to / settle your claim for the errors and delays in repairing / your door and gates and replacing some glass. We have / the total sum of $296 / which you will recall you settled with us in March. / In answer to your note, two boxes of glasses, cups, / mugs, and plates will be sent to you on the / railway as the road may be unsafe for such things. / Pay the total sum and in a month, you will / be able to claim our bonus of four per cent. / We also enclose a note of two lots of metal / chairs and tables we bought in the market a month / ago. **(121)**

(b) Standard

Part of the cargo on a vessel in B dock / exploded. A large blaze glowed for some hours, and a / pall of smoke lay in the air. As a result, / the port had to close. All on board the vessel / were told to go ashore, and the dock was vacated / except for those who were left to take the vessels / in the docks on to the lake. We expect to / have local reports today and we will be able to / get you some added facts. The vessel has sunk and / is regarded as a total loss. **(96)**

We are waiting for the labels for the sets of / plates that we have manufactured for you. As you know, / they are in two colours and although some delay is / expected in getting the shade of yellow you chose, we / will be able to purchase them all this month. We / are having the plates laid at places on old elm / tables. The watches and clocks for show will be on / large oak settles along with the gold plate. We also / have some models of boats in black glass to show. / It is safe to say it will be a marked / success and large sales ought to follow. **(107)**

(c) Standard

We make ropes and cables and a customer, who has / bought a lot of our work, sent us your name. / May we manufacture for you? We are able to make / anything of any length, weight and shape in rope, metal / or glass for your purposes. We enclose photos of some / of our rope-walks which also show our methods of / manufacture for world markets. We claim to do nothing but / top-class work for all our customers and our rates / for making any ropes or cables you select will be / as low as any. May we come and talk to / you to tell you all the facts? The customers' remarks / which are enclosed will show you that our ample claims / are not false. **(123)**

At some places on the edges of the lake are / shells of rare shapes and shades of colour that resemble / glass. The shells are left on the shoals and banks / as the lake is low this month. You may get / them for yourself but you will have to take the / boat with a spade and bucket or satchel to pack / them in. Take care. The lake is noted for its / swell. Sail back to the bay to escape the swell / supposing you get caught in it. **(86)**

4 THEORY CHECKS

clay	clutch	settled	angle
gamble	block	ample	arable
pledge	chapel	battle	parable
globe	supple	vocal	claimed
rubble	clothing	paddle	plod

5 FREE DICTATION

Some of the cases of things we sent for export / are waiting to go on a boat in the docks. / This is the loading form. Will you locate them for / us and have them sent to us on the railway? / We have to replace some of the glass tops of / the tables for our customers in Glasgow and this could / take us a day or two to do. They all / go on board the vessel 'Thomas Clark' which sails on / Monday. We shall have to rush them to the port / on the car for loading and pack them in cases / ourselves. **(101)**

SECTION 6
UNIT 10
of Pitman 2000 First Course

1 SHORT FORM PRACTICE

(*a*)

immediately	should	without	influence
largest	immediate	influencing	also
influenced	several	first	almost
always	owed	owing	owes
ought	owe	are	largely
first	influence	several	almost
influencing	immediate	should	influenced
immediately	able to	largest	without
who	large	dollar	had
on	shall	which	would
could	manufacturing	yours	manufacturer
thanked	yesterday	our	your
has	we	too	to
is	the	immediate	immediately
manufactured	yourself	manufactures	an

(*b*)

(i) We should buy several of-the largest items immediately. (**9**)

(ii) We-are almost without any influence with-the buyers. (**9**)

(iii) The first of-several cases should-be with-you almost immediately. (**11**)

(iv) Almost our first task will-be to-get an immediate stock of-the largest items. (**15**)

(v) Several changes in-the-market are influencing buyers and-they-will-be influenced by-the stocks of-manufacturers without-which several of-them may fail. (**25**)

2 PHRASES

I will, I am, I came, I like, I may, for the first time, first class, just as, as fast as, as the, as much as, at first, bank charges, store charge, stock forms, tax forms, it was, it was not, we will charge, they will form.

3 DICTATION

(a) Easy

I am glad to know that you like some of / the items of baggage we have sent to you. We / are able to supply them in several styles and it / is just the time to buy as costs are low / this month. Most of the bags and cases are supplied / in several sizes and we suggest that the largest are / those that will sell well. We are also enclosing two / large posters for your shop. **(75)**

Make the best of your time. This is the wise / thing to do. The clock does not stop, and the / hours lost are lost for always. Do the exercise you / ought to do today and not tomorrow. Ask yourself 'Am / I doing my best?' This applies to work just as / much as to play. Most of us do our best / sometimes but we should aim to do our best always. / **(70)**

We are delighted to know that Tom Pike will be / in charge of the designs for the cloth we are / making for our large markets in China. It is a / wise choice. Tom knows China well, passed some of his / life in that part of the world, and was awarded / the Red Star medal for all his work in making / first-class manufactured light-weight cloth for the markets of / China. Tom might be going to China to get the / right styles and colours. **(84)**

(b) Standard

Some of the employees have just lost wages because supplies / of manufactured items made for us by firms we rely / on could not be sent to us. They say it / is unavoidable. They have exhausted the stocks which came to / them by boat and the stoppage of work in the / docks is the cause of the long delays. Most of / our employees have worked for us for a long time / past and they expect us to pay them. We say / we will not lay them off but we will pay / them just for the work they do. The loss of / stocks is not our fault. In this state of affairs / we should welcome your advice. **(115)**

We have large stocks of plates, cups, saucers and glasses, / and such items which we bought several months ago. The / Armed Forces Supply Depot asked us to suggest a sum / for cash sale of four large lots A to

D. / They accepted our low charge as the best and we / had the space to take all the lots at the / same time. So we are able to let you have / first-class supplies of the items, all of them tested, / at a cost not to be matched as long as / they last. We suggest you post us the form today. / (**100**)

(c) **Standard**

We make up surfaces in all types of stone, but / most of all in alabaster and marble in which we / do our best work, not to be surpassed by any. / Our employees are all experts and they come to us / because we are the oldest firm doing this work. We / were licensed by Edward III and authorised to get our / stone in the west, close to Chester. We have our / ways of colouring alabaster and marble and of making stone / surfaces like glass which we defy any to match. We / apologise for the boast, but our work justifies it as / we will show you. (**104**)

Cobbett's rides in the shires exposed much that was wrong—/the way that honest peasants could be arrested, and the / waste, that was largely the support in life of the / peasants, enclosed to make fields. At the same time, his / writings tell us of the life of his times and / they may be read to be enjoyed today. Cobbett spoke / for the working classes of his age. (**67**)

We are sending you by post today fifty-two of / the alloy coils you asked us for yesterday. The rest—/that is eighteen alloy castings—will be sent by rail / but we shall not be able to do this by / Monday next. Will Wednesday be in time for you? Will / you let us know immediately as we have a customer / waiting for them? (**63**)

4 THEORY CHECKS

climb	Ulster	voyagers	Chesterfield
knife	coasts	estate	endings
toiling	ripest	arise	rejoice
adjust	tide	sausages	riots
silence	digested	paymaster	knight

5 FREE DICTATION

In the last two months we have had to meet / rises in costs both in manufactures and in the wages / of our employees. Passing on some of this large cost / to our customers is unavoidable and we are taking steps / to let our customers know of this next month. Some / fall in our sales is expected but we shall do / our best to get export markets for our light metal / alloy rakes which are the finest in the world. / (**79**)

SECTION 7
UNIT 11
of Pitman 2000 First Course

1 SHORT FORM PRACTICE

(a)

dear	larger	I	trade
the	and	according	do
towards	is	you	any
it	of	in	toward
particular	to	is	thing
toward	have	trade	this
anything	larger	something	all
for	nothing	dear	thank
according to	be	being	accord
towards	with	that	as
has	but	will	we
immediate	should	largest	your
without	immediately	first	thanking
influence	influenced	our	an
several	almost	influencing	his

(b)

(i) According-to our trade reports this particular type is too-dear. **(11)**
(ii) Nothing larger is in stock and-this type is-the largest wę-have. **(13)**
(iii) We-shall go towards-the lake, but-we-will take particular care. **(12)**
(iv) Several of-the larger items which-are dear should-be traded in. **(12)**
(v) Send-us-the first items immediately, in particular, the largest that-you have. **(13)**

2 PHRASES

Dear Sir, yours faithfully, yours sincerely, of course, at some time, for some time, for the first time, first class, I regret, I recorded, I am, I will, in the course of, just as, this is, as fast as, on the, is the, was the, has the, but the, with such.

3 DICTATION

(a) Easy

At present the price of paper is too dear for / us to buy much and this is a problem as / our stocks are low. Our buyers tell us that in / a month or two larger supplies of paper will become / available and the price will fall. We trust that by / October we shall be able to buy all we desire / at better prices, that our stocks will last, and that / our forecasts of supplies will be correct. We have no / labour problems at this time, as we pay the best / rates of any in the trade for all grades of / workers in paper. **(103)**

We have just purchased two branch shops and both of / them have the best sites for sales. They are in / Exeter and in Chester. They will sell paper and anything / for art work and writing. I am enclosing the addresses / for you. Will you try to get across to see / them in the next month? I regret to tell you / that I am unable to go because, as I expect / you remember, I have to go straight to Manchester to / take on labour to raise the manufacture of our paper / products. Our sales of this type of item, it is / safe to say, will grow, and we must take steps / to get in stocks for our customers. **(117)**

(b) Standard

Our employees on this estate enjoy the best rates of / pay. We supply them with large cottages for which they / pay nothing, and we have a shop on the estate / selling a great range of things at low cost. In / October, we prepare a great spread for our Cider Supper / and they all come to this—adults, boys, girls and / babes. We are delighted to supply prizes and presents for / all who come. They work well for us and we / express our thanks to them in this way. Of course, / they all get a bonus in December too. It is / not surprising that we are able to attract the best / workers, and it is nice that we are able to / say that we have no labour problems. **(127)**

According to the court records of the past in the / law courts at Exeter, this estate has belonged to the / Chesters for a long time. They first appeared in the / records as long ago as 1367 and they / bought the estate, which was small at the time, in / the Wars of the Roses in 1462. In / the course of time they added much to it, and / enclosed a large acreage for growing crops. They also added / to its size by buying the forest next to it, / some of which has survived up to the present day, / though most was cut for charcoal or for making trading / vessels for the fast-growing trade of the west. Success / in farming the soil of this estate made the great / wealth of the Chesters and they became famous for methods / of growing the largest crops of oats and potatoes. (**149**)

(c) Standard

Dear Sir, You asked us some time ago to send / you some of our knives and forks, cups, plates and / saucers, and you suggested to us that you might be / buying large numbers of them for your customers in Canada. / This was some months ago and on 8 December last / we sent you a note of the sum for the / boxes of items sent, and we stressed that the debt / should be settled in a month. We have waited for / your cheque expecting to have it any day but we / have had nothing. A note is enclosed stating the total / sum. May we ask you to pay immediately as we / are loth to place the case in the care of / our lawyers. We should like it much better were we / able to supply you with such items for your market. / Yours faithfully, (**142**)

Dear Tom, I will expect you, as you suggest, at / the Forum next Wednesday and I should be arriving by / five o'clock. I note that you are to address the / members on 'Destroying Pests', and I know that they will / be glad to have your expert advice on this. I / expect you are talking of crop pests though we both / know some types not among crops, do we not, that / might well be destroyed? My joke of course! Up to / the present one hundred and seventy-four have said they / will be coming. They will all be members of local / farming clubs. Yours sincerely, Jack. (**105**)

4 THEORY CHECKS

fibre	occurrence	branches	strike
addresses	subscribe	ancestor	water
expressing	August	scattered	correct
spray	poacher	across	collect
treble	ledger	draw	scraped

5 FREE DICTATION

The present price of copper which we make up in / a large number of types of metal casings and pipes / is not low, but as it is probable that it / will rise, we are aiming to raise our stocks of / copper blocks. We buy them in Canada and they are / brought by boat to our dock in Glasgow. Our market / may well grow in the months to come as our / sales charts show that a rise may be expected. We / shall be able to take in larger stocks of copper / in a month or two because we are getting space / to store the copper blocks in our branch depot in / Manchester. We shall have enough labour available for the work / we will have to do. **(125)**

SECTION 8
UNIT 12
of Pitman 2000 First Course

Tape available

1 SHORT FORM PRACTICE

(*a*)

think	put	putting	to be
puts	larger	dear	year
particular	towards	trade	according to
without	influence	largest	several
influenced	also	influencing	always
year	put	putting	thinks
puts	owed	owes	owe
ought	are	able to	largely
large	dollar	on	shall
had	could	manufacturing	manufacture
manufactured	manufacturer	thank	to
thanked	yesterday	yours	today
thinking	put	year	years
trade	puts	to be	putting
although	towards	particular	it

(*b*)

(i) Do-you think-this should-be put in this year? (**10**)

(ii) Trade this year is, according-to reports, likely to-be larger in-several particular items. (**15**)

(iii) The manufacturers think-that-the larger items ought-to-be put first in-the list. (**15**)

(iv) We-are putting the sums owed last-year towards this year's debt. (**12**)

(v) Thank-you for thinking of-us yesterday. We-will-do our best to-be-present at-the next meeting. (**19**)

2 PHRASES

this business, your business, our business, large business, manufacturing business, I think, I thank, we think, in this city, this is, has to be, is to be, ought to be, if we, if we are, if we were, if you are, if they are, if they were, yours faithfully, yours sincerely, at some time, at the same time.

3 DICTATION

(a) Easy

Dear Sirs, We are sending back to you today a / large chest of Mills' Family Tea. Regrettably it has become / spoiled by coming into close touch with oil and this, / as we suggest in the report, may possibly have occurred / in its transport by ship. We spoke to your depot / yesterday and they have already sent us a chest of / tea to replace that which we are unable to use. / This, we are told, will be India tea grade 2, / and we shall need a credit note because of the / lower price of this tea. Yours faithfully, **(97)**

Our business is not large yet people come daily into / our area to shop and in particular to pay money, / not just for things like radios, food, shoes and clothing, / which we all must have, but for artistic items. We / have tried to build this business on our belief that / we could succeed in appealing to the desire many show, / of being ready to invest money to get serious and / agreeable works of art that they feel able to live / with. Statistics are showing that we were clearly right. Because / of the obvious success of artistic items, we are soon / going to add jewels and rings to our list of / goods for sale. **(113)**

(b) Standard

We thank you for all you are doing for us / in the move of our office premises to Leeds, and / for setting up our large factory in the West Riding / in the year just past. May we ask you if / you are able to take on the task of transporting / four hundred and sixty-two tables, filing cabinets, office chairs / and carpets which, according to estimates, will need twenty-five / lorries to be available for any two days in the / period 4th to 15th September of this year. We are / aware that your charges will have to be increased because / of the rising costs of oil and labour. If this / seems to be possible we should welcome a meeting with / you to go into the business in detail. Will you / please get in touch with us? **(136)**

(c) Standard

If you aim just for speed in typing, the number / of errors made is sure to increase. If you aim / to type without making any mistakes, your speed will fall. / The two things will not work at the same time. / It is better to teach people to type first for / correct striking of the keys and for speed, and next / to type with the simple aim of a faultless result. / To reach success in both aims they must be practised, / changing goals several times in a period of fifteen or / sixteen minutes. In business and in office work we have / to bring the two goals into a single aim of / fast but correct typing. As you practise, it is always / best to keep the two apart as much as possible. / **(130)**

Dear Mr Peel, We wish to inform you that we / have succeeded in getting the lease of your factory building / signed today, a day or two early. This will make / it possible for you to start shifting all the larger / items on to the premises immediately. Please let us know / which of the office systems you wish to install and / inform us, by telex, of the time the first lorries / will arrive. Your copy of the list is enclosed dated / 31 July. Yours sincerely, **(85)**

I should be glad if you would send me some / facts dealing with your scheme to increase the supply of / your goods to those districts in the West in which / you have sales to the large shops and stores. It / would assist us in making our report to the Board / on sales progress for the coming period. **(57)**

4 THEORY CHECKS

cool	premium	successive	stinging
pity	liberal	statistics	cheapest
zero	skill	feared	trick
instead	boots	mild	steep
insert	spring	poodle	figure

5 FREE DICTATION

Dear Sir, You wrote to us in May asking us / to supply you daily with papers and magazines and you / wrote a full list of all you wished us to / send. We started according to your wishes on 14 May. / Today is 22 July and though we have sent / you several bills in this period, you have not to / date paid any money or got in touch with us. / Enclosed is a bill for the total sum that is / owed to date. In a small business like ours, we / are unable to let customers have long credit, and we / must ask you to pay in cash or by cheque / in a week. If not, we shall with regret be / obliged to start legal proceedings to get the debt settled. / Yours faithfully, **(132)**

SECTION 9
UNIT 13
of Pitman 2000 First Course

1 SHORT FORM PRACTICE

(*a*)

large	how	do	nothing
and	subject	in	for
of	his	subjected	have
to	I	thing	subjecting
today	you	any	be
subject	anything	subjected	being
too	large	something	with
that	this	all	subjecting
has	particular	will	thanking
but	without	according to	to be

(*b*)

(i) Thank-you for anything you-may-have on-this-subject. (**10**)
(ii) How is this-subject to-be dealt-with today if anything is said? (**13**)
(iii) We-shall-be subjecting ourselves to-something we-know nothing of. (**11**)
(iv) Has-the subject of how we-are all to-get to-the boat arisen? (**14**)
(v) He subjected us today to-his usual chatter about nothing. (**10**)

2 PHRASES

I hope, we hope, I hope you are, we hope you will, he is, he has the, he will, he will be, if he, if he is, if he will, as he, as he is, this is, this subject, on this subject, for this subject, I think he is, we think he will, is he, if he is the, in this business, entry forms, bank charges, it is to be.

3 DICTATION

(a) Easy

It was announced at the meeting that all workers in / the power-houses would get rises of 12½ / per cent, and this the crowd of several thousands in / the Tower Building greeted with loud cheers. They had said / earlier that they might go on strike if they could / not get better wages. No doubt the newspapers will report / all the facts tomorrow and we have asked Jack Hope / to write a review of the whole history of the / dispute. I hope he will be as fair and just / as he usually is in his writing. Few press writers / could do better. **(103)**

Dear Ted, It was good to hear your voice today. / We hope that if you are in this neighbourhood next / month you will call in to see us. We shall / be happy to put you up, so you will not / have to pay high hotel prices. Make it a holiday / for a day or two. This is a healthy place / with good wholesome air, and we have several first-class / golf courses here. We have a large double garage and / perhaps you could bring Anne with you, too. We see / too little of you both these days. I shall be / in the office on Tuesday. Will you ring me at / four o'clock? Yours as always, Dick. **(116)**

(b) Standard

We think that if we set up our factory in / the south of the country we are likely to get / a higher output per hour and a larger volume of / manufactured goods. In that area we should have fewer labour / problems, and we should also save on the cost of / transport. We should be twenty-seven miles nearer all the / services we shall need, and to the principal markets for / our goods. For these reasons we suggest that we should / call the Board for an early meeting making the Hilltop / Hotel our venue. If you agree, I presume you would / wish me to secure a large room and also to / make sure of lunch and bar facilities. **(117)**

Dear Sirs, We shall in a short time start a / bureau in your area of the city in the High / Street. Our aim is to cater for all types of / copying, stencil, and offset work and to set up a / speedy service coupled with high grade output. We enclose a / rate card and, as you will see, our prices are / the lowest in the neighbourhood and indeed in the whole /

country. Also we are installing a hire service for most / copying devices, and for some temporary help in typing at / heavy load times as, for example, in the holiday period. / We also enclose samples of our work. We shall be / happy to do any job on trial. Yours faithfully, (**119**)

(c) **Standard**

The subject of this book is health and it has / much of value to say to us in particular about / health on holiday. We are advised to keep out of / the heat and to protect ourselves should the sun be / too hot if we wish to keep well. Unusual food / and drink should be avoided except in hotels. If swimming / is part of the holiday the hair ought to be / washed or shampooed each day or two. It is better / to take less food if the holiday is not too / strenuous and fewer drinks also, at least during the day, / except for soft drinks. Our reviewer suggests that the book / is first-class value for money. (**116**)

This individual memo is to inform you about our move / to Reading at the end of next month. Work in / all offices will end on Tuesday, 17 July, and all / books, records, and files will be moved first, places for / them already being fixed in the new premises. All members / of staff will be allowed two days clear for removing / to the houses allocated and for settling in. The firm / will pay the total cost of the move with the / cost of all meals during the two days. Fully-fitted / carpets will be laid for you according to the choice / you made some weeks ago and this will be carried / out two days earlier. Work will start at 1130 / hours on Monday, 23 July. Ask Mr Harris about / any particular problems you may have. (**136**)

4 THEORY CHECKS

heal	crouch	livelihood	bough
bout	helpless	accurate	crowded
feud	refusing	hamper	towel
unduly	assumes	due	Haig
secure	mirage	harbour	manhood

5 FREE DICTATION

On the hire purchase debt you are due to pay / the first sum next month, and the rest each month / on the first day of the month of the two-/year period. We suggest that you should insure your colour / TV set immediately and that you should also take out / our Upkeep Policy so that any fault may be corrected / or spare part replaced straight away. If any fault arises / and is reported by midday, service is always available on / the same day, Saturdays and Sundays (but not Bank Holidays) / included. Our upkeep and service is of great value to / you. (**101**)

SECTION 10
UNIT 14
of Pitman 2000 First Course

1 SHORT FORM PRACTICE

(a)

cannot	to be	subjected	thanked
subject	responsible	your	manufacture
put	puts	responsibility	yours
gentlemen	year	yesterday	gentleman
putting	how	yourself	subjecting
particularly	responsibility	could	large
how	cannot	on	who
responsible	manufacturer	gentleman	largely
subject	shall	had	gentlemen
accordingly	which	dollar	able to

(b)

(i) Of-course I-cannot-be responsible for-this-subject which-should-be yours. **(13)**

(ii) It-is-the responsibility of a gentleman to-think of-his fellows. **(12)**

(iii) These gentlemen have particularly asked to-be put on-your list as-soon-as-possible. **(15)**

(iv) This year I-wish you to-take responsibility for a large-department. **(12)**

(v) I-cannot-be responsible for-the safety of-these gentlemen, particularly since yesterday's happenings. **(14)**

2 PHRASES

you can, you cannot, I can, I cannot, we cannot, I am not, I will not, we will not, it will not, I want, I wanted, I regret, I regretted, at once, we hope, I hope, I hope you will not, it has been, we will arrange, we have arranged, this arrangement, sales department, accounts department, wholesale department, retail department, Fire Department, had not, did not, do not.

3 DICTATION

(a) Easy

Unless we can get the machines and the plant installed / in the factory by March, we shall be able to / produce only 57 per cent of your needs in / manufactured goods by the end of the year, even though / we are ready to pay our men higher rates for / the job. In any case machines need much maintenance in / the early stages and we may find that, because of / this, it will not be easy for us to attain / even these goals. We do not wish to disappoint you / by promising something we cannot carry out. So we look / to you to help us to ensure that the machines / are in place in the factory and ready for use / some time in March. **(124)**

Dear Sir, We will soon be announcing to the public / our annual sale of genuine bargains in all kinds of / cotton, woollen and man-made textiles for the trade. But / as one of our oldest customers we wish you to / have first choice of the many bargains in large lots / of cloth that are available, so we have arranged for / our sales department to visit you by arrangement with you / to show you a large range of samples. The list / of these with the prices at which we can sell / them is enclosed. Will you please telephone us to make / an appointment? We hope you will not mind accepting our / terms of cash settlement within one month of purchase. Yours / faithfully, **(121)**

(b) Standard

Someone once said that all political rule is bad. The / point is that those with the power are all human / and so they must all have weaknesses. Unfortunately, we have / to put up with the bad and balance it against / the good. As the same person added, we can only / make up our minds between them on the grounds of / how bad they are, because we soon learn that if / we expect much of any regime we are certain to / be disappointed. This is particularly so in democracies which depend / greatly on the intelligence of the people and how well / they are informed about affairs. Even in a country like / ours in which schools and colleges abound, many hold the / view that the power of the uninformed and the less / intelligent is too great. But if you do not want / a democracy then you must face the problem of deciding / on some form of rule to replace it which will / be better. Nobody yet has come up with the answer. / (**170**)

Dear Mr Jones, I regret that you have had some / delay in the settlement of your account for expenses for / May and June. These have been agreed and a cheque / in payment is enclosed. You will be pleased to hear / that we recently had a telephone call with Dunster and / Sons in Brighton and they spoke highly of the work / you had done for them on your visit in June. / We have had several similar talks with firms in the / South, and evidently because of your work our goods are / becoming increasingly well-known. Thank you for all you are / doing. Yours sincerely, (**103**)

(c) **Standard**

The Fire Department of this city write to remind us / that it is time to examine again the steps we / take to ensure the safety of all staff in the / event of fire. The Fire Department have made several suggestions / about our existing arrangements and also they demand that we / hold fire drills. In the coming month we shall, without / previous announcement, hold two fire drills at various times of / the day. All members of staff are to study the / enclosed fire drill arrangements with care and put them into / practice immediately the alarm bell is rung. (**97**)

Dear Sir, Our business is to finance firms like your / own which need to buy land, or machines, or mining / rights to expand output. As the enclosed documents will show / you, we can certainly supply the means by which you / can extend your business on better terms than those of / the banks. Knowing that you are at the moment thinking / of trying to extend your interests in the south-western / part of the region, we should be glad of the / chance to call upon your Accounts Department to discuss the / ways in which we might well be of help to / you. Yours faithfully, (**103**)

4 THEORY CHECKS

adjourn	trend	vain	stolen
chanced	eventually	adorn	dispensed
plain	vans	burning	amusement
engines	romances	silence	chains
lions	agent	happening	attainment

5 FREE DICTATION

I regret that we cannot dispatch this week the bed / you bought two months ago. We are sorry to disappoint / you but we are having great trouble in obtaining supplies / and even if we were able to get all we / wanted, we are still short of the skilled men and / women needed to reduce the heavy backlog of work. We / hope to install a second machine for cutting joints next / week, and if we do not run into any problems / with service and maintenance, we should be able to dispatch / your bed with the fittings as arranged in about twenty-/one days. We are sincerely sorry to put you to / this trouble, and our sales department is sending you a / credit note as a token of our regret. **(128)**

SECTION 11
UNIT 15
of Pitman 2000 First Course

1 SHORT FORM PRACTICE

(*a*)

cannot	satisfactory	before	are
together	responsible	from	ought
very	altogether	responsibility	owe
gentlemen	their	commercial	gentleman
particularly	more	manufactured	always
gentlemen	particularly	altogether	responsible
responsibility	cannot	gentleman	satisfactory
together	very	before	commercially
there	more	from	should
owing	also	immediate	without

(*b*)

(i) Our commercial books have-had very-satisfactory results in-the past year. (**12**)

(ii) There-are-more from-the towns who-will-be coming in very-soon. (**13**)

(iii) He-was-not altogether a bad man before he lost his responsible job. (**13**)

(iv) From our sales records it-seems there-are very few more customers this year than last. (**16**)

(v) If-we work together from-the start, we should-have a satisfactory result commercially. (**14**)

2 PHRASES

there is, there are, there will be, there are no, there is no, more than, better than, higher than, taller than, have been, we have been, should have been, had been, I had been, do not, had not, very much, very little, how much, it is certain, I cannot, I am not, I regret, it will not, you are not, at once, for the first time, did not, lower than, I have been, our own, your own.

3 DICTATION

(a) Easy

Dear Sirs, We have been through the accounts with care / to try to find the difference which you pointed out / last week. However, although we have been over each statement, / we have had no success. Will you please let us / have more details from your Accounts Department, otherwise we have / no way of discovering the error or errors? Perhaps it / would be best if we arranged for two clerks from / each of our two firms to meet with all the / documents to go over them together. If this is satisfactory / to you, please telephone us. Yours faithfully, (**97**)

In the summer when the weather is good, it is / a pleasure to sit by the river in the shade / of the trees and pass one's leisure in the lovely / gardens of this old manor. In the pressure and stress / of business life, we forget how it feels to be / free and to savour the joys of the open air, / and enjoy the many art treasures of our fine old / country houses. So many of them open both their gardens / and their rooms to us in the best months of / the year. They all offer us so much at such / a low cost that we ought to go to see / them more often than we do. (**116**)

(b) Standard

Every year more of our business is taken up by / the food side. I am glad to tell you that / our sales show most satisfactory increases. We have this year / put in three new deep-freezing plants at our factories / in Cheshire. I am sure that much of our success / results from our steady policy of obtaining only the finest / foods. In particular our canned fruits and frozen vegetables grow / more popular each season. We are now offered the largest / bread-baking unit in Europe, and the Board takes a / favourable view of the offer, and proposes to cater for / a great present need, and that is a loaf of / bread made from the whole grain with nothing added. It / is our purpose to cash in on the protest of / so many people against the present loaf so often lacking / in savour and nourishment. (**144**)

Dear Mr Driver, Last summer I was on holiday in / your area and visited your estate, and there I bought / shrubs and plants which I am glad to tell you / have been first-class and have produced a much greater / than average number of blooms. These we have been able / to gather for display in the house, and they have / attracted much favourable notice from our friends and neighbours. Would / you now please send me your latest catalogue and price-/list as I would like to buy a fresh supply / for planting in May? Yours sincerely, (**96**)

(c) **Standard**

Many people have an itch to write but not many / succeed at it. There is some advice we can offer / from experience which may be of use. The first thing / is to make sure that you are familiar with the / ways in which sentences are put together. Remember that there / are many more ways of saying things than just by / stringing them together with 'and' or 'but'. By subordinating one / idea to the other and thinking about the right place / for words and phrases you can very often do much / better. Vary the length of your sentences too. Be short / and simple, but take care not to have too many / short snappy sentences at one time chattering away like machine / guns. Try to use fewer words because too many may / cloud your meaning instead of making it sharper. Make certain / that your meaning is clear and think of the person / who has to read the article or essay you have / written. Do not be afraid of using words that appeal / to the senses, thus bringing colour and life to your / message. (**181**)

Dear Sir, Silver has always been one of the minerals / that brings most pleasure to men and women. We are / workers in silver and have been so since 1754./ We feel sure that you will find the enclosed / brochure of interest, particularly as we know of your purchases / of silver plate in the last few years. We make / fine copies of any antique silver objects that are almost / impossible to tell apart from the genuine ones. Yours faithfully, / (**80**)

4 THEORY CHECKS

average	rather	coffers	freely
difference	everyone	favourable	framed
diner	otherwise	versatile	throughout
funeral	France	hover	threads
weather	Friday	weaver	either

5 FREE DICTATION

We read either to inform ourselves or to enjoy ourselves. / Sometimes the two aims come together at the same time / as, if we look up a word to find out / its meaning, we discover in a few minutes that we / are reading on about other words because it is all / so interesting. The range of facts today is so tremendous / that no one man could possibly master them all. For / this reason we need to have encyclopaedias arranged in some / regular way so that we can find out speedily all / we need to know. On the other hand, we can / if we wish settle down with a book that suits / our taste and transport ourselves into a different world for / hours at a time. **(124)**

SECTION 12
UNIT 16
of Pitman 2000 First Course

1 SHORT FORM PRACTICE

(a)

enlarge	satisfactory	more	influencing
influential	enlarged	their	largest
altogether	very	enlarger	almost
before	commercial	owed	enlargement
from	immediately	influence	several
together	enlarged	enlarge	dear
enlarging	particularly	first	larger
influential	owes	manufacturing	according
influenced	enlargement	particular	trade
to be	put	think	towards

(b)

(i) This enlarger makes a very-good enlargement from a particularly small photo. (**12**)

(ii) Almost all-the commercial and manufacturing people here seek to enlarge their influence in-this particular trade. (**17**)

(iii) Trade with-these parts is influenced and enlarged by-the largest commercial firms. (**13**)

(iv) The more we-work together, the more influential we-shall-be in enlarging our trade. (**15**)

(v) Our first choice was altogether too-dear and-several people advised us that-it-should-be put on sale again immediately. (**21**)

2 PHRASES

several months, this month, some months, as soon as, as soon as possible, as early as possible, it is possible, it is not possible, as soon as we can, these arrangements, this form, more than, we have been, better than, retail department, we regret, I will not, I can, I am, I regret.

3 DICTATION

(a) Easy

We hope to travel for several months across Africa. We / shall go part of the way by car and part / by camel or on foot. Our purpose is to seek / out new species of flowers. You might think on the / face of it that, because the largest part of Africa / is well-known, it is not possible to find new / flowers, but the truth is that new ones are still / found and the facts about botany are added to almost / every year. Only a year ago a famous botanist brought / back no fewer than five flowers from the Hope Range / of hills, which no man in Europe at least had / ever seen before. **(113)**

Dear Sir, May we remind you that the books we / asked you to dispatch on 13 May have still not / yet been delivered here, although we have telephoned you three / times and this is the second note that we have / written on the subject? We have been told that the / books are not out of stock and that they have / been available without a break for some years past. Perhaps / you would please explain the long delay for which there / seems no reason. We are hopeful that you will now / make a special effort to supply us. Yours faithfully, **(99)**

(b) Standard

The supply of fresh water free from injurious forms of / life and pure enough to drink with safety is an / essential of urban planning. In fact it is well known / that ample supplies of good water, not only for drinking, / but for all the many other purposes for which it / is vital, is a first call on all local and / regional resources. Here in this country we are fortunate to / have plenty of rain, but the number of people goes / on rising and the amount of water that each person / uses has risen sharply in the last few years. This / is because larger volumes of water are used by industry, / and people use much more than they used to for / showers, bathing and car washing. Increasing amounts are used for / main drains and sewage. Have you ever thought, for instance, / of the vast supply of water that is used just / for the one purpose of flushing our cisterns millions of / times each day—one hundred and forty-three millions it / is estimated. Modern pump cisterns would need only one tenth / of this and a great economy in both water and / money could be effected. **(194)**

Dear Mr Tanner, I am glad to hear that such / a beautiful bouquet of flowers arrived safely and in time / for Jane's birthday. I was not able to choose them / myself as I was travelling at the time, but I / left it to my assistant who is a marvel at / this kind of thing. We look forward to seeing you / at the week-end. Yours sincerely, (**66**)

(c) **Standard**

Dear Sir, We submit for your approval our plan for / your travel to India and Malaysia next month. Would you / please let us know as soon as you can if / the arrangements are satisfactory, and in any case telephone us / before Saturday, as we have to make the final arrangements / by 24th June to be sure of getting all / the hotel and airways booked. Please send a deposit of / 12½ per cent of the total sum / due. The balance may be paid upon your return, but / we shall send you a statement in due course. Please / note, also, that you must have been inoculated against yellow / fever and have been vaccinated against small-pox within the / last three years. Yours truly, (**125**)

The plan to move from our present offices in Victoria / to the new block in Camden has had to be / put off for a time. It is still proposed to / move as soon as possible, and as we think this / is almost sure to be within a week or two, / you are now expected to act upon Plan C, and / all officials for the move at the level of Department / Heads or higher, should take all the necessary steps to / have all items included in Plan C packed and ready / for immediate removal. (**93**)

4 THEORY CHECKS

helpful	reflect	flames	thrive
especial	marshal	liver	differing
rivalry	enamel	skilful	cipher
novelist	tunnel	fragrance	however
panelled	flickering	sinful	clever

5 FREE DICTATION

There are other ways of sending messages as well as / by the familiar signs of the alphabet we learn at / infant school written or typed on paper. It was Samuel / Morse, an American art teacher, who in 1837 / invented a code revised in 1844, of dots / and dashes to stand for the alphabetic signs. Those occurring / most often were assigned short forms such as a single / dot for E and three dots for S. For a / century this code was used on line and then on / radio. Louis Braille at about the same time invented the / system of raised dots on thick paper which remains without / rival as a system enabling the blind to enjoy reading / and follow a musical score with the tips of the / fingers. (**131**)

SECTION 13
UNIT 17
of Pitman 2000 First Course

1 SHORT FORM PRACTICE

(*a*)

satisfactory	before	commercially	year
difficult	altogether	enlarge	how
together	thankful	influential	subject
very	more	putting	cannot
there	from	enlarger	responsible
enlarged	particular	difficulty	gentleman
puts	together	the	thankful
subjected	satisfactory	it	of
responsibility	altogether	and	particularly
enlargement	gentlemen	is	subjecting

(*b*)

(i) I-am thankful to-learn that-this year things have-not-been more difficult. (**14**)

(ii) It-is your responsibility to achieve a much more satisfactory result, gentlemen! (**12**)

(iii) We-were very thankful to-be together again as-we-had-been subjected to a difficult test. (**17**)

(iv) I-will-not enlarge upon this difficult subject particularly as-it-is time to-go. (**15**)

(v) We get more and enlarged responsibilities from-the beginning of-the-year, and our difficulties increase. (**16**)

2 PHRASES

out of, part of, type of, lack of, short of, number of, member of, instead of, in spite of, rate of, state of, group of, sort of, who have, ought to have, which have, who have not, who have not been, you have.

3 DICTATION

(a) Easy

If you can let me have an advance of £2,000 / for a brief time, I shall be able / to make a profit within a month on the sale / of the goods I buy, and I am ready to / give you ten per cent of this. This will be / to the advantage of us both. If you agree, I / hope it may be kept as a private arrangement. There / is nothing that is not legal and proper about the / scheme, but I think we should act on our own / behalf in the first instance. If the market develops as / I think it will, then we can provide for shares / in the scheme for our relatives. Although I wish to / take the first risk, once we know we have a / good market, I am ready to make a half share / agreement with you and bring in three or four on / each side to enlarge the range of our dealings. (**159**)

This note gives us nothing positive to work on. We / cannot tell from reading it if we are expected to / draft a report on the regional sales, or just to / observe which are the best selling lines and who are / the salesmen representing us best at this time. I think / we should ask for something more definite. (**57**)

(b) Standard

A problem always with us is that of traffic in / the towns. You have only to drive through any large / city to find out for yourself. Many local councils seek / to preserve some areas for pedestrians and shopping and to / defend their cities from the growing threat of the car / and the heavy van. They very rightly devote time and / money to the defence of their streets and they deserve / to succeed. Much has been achieved already, but it will / prove difficult to prevent the car from dominating our lives. / Some rough measures will be necessary before the problem is / solved. (**101**)

Dear Sir, I was very pleased to receive the gift / only two days from the date I posted the coupons. / The silver cups are really beautiful and they will be / useful both for wine and as highly attractive items in / my display cabinet. I gather from the enclosed note that / I have a credit of one hundred coupons. I now / enclose by registered mail one thousand coupons and, as you / will see, I have filled in a new form for / the porcelain tea set (Number 23) in red and / gold. Will you please note also the change of address / as above. Yours truly, **(104)**

(c) Standard

We are sorry that our arrangements for servicing cloakrooms and / toilets have not been as effective as we would have / wished in the past few months. There have been a / number of different reasons for this, in particular a lack / of staff and changes of duties among supervisory employees. The / problem is now solved and new towel machines have been / installed on all four floors with a regular supply of / hot water for all wash basins, together with soap, brushes / and other toilet articles and items. In the event of / any trouble, members of staff are asked to telephone Tom / Evans or his assistant on house telephone 249. / **(110)**

Dear Miss Lever, We have received from you the draft / art sketches you did for the cover of our new / title 'Perfect Wives'. You will be pleased to hear, I / am sure, that all of us here regard them as / highly original and beautifully and strikingly drawn. They fit the / main topics ideally, and there is no doubt that they / will add much to the impact of the book which / will be published in three months on 14 July. On / behalf of the Board I send you our thanks, and / enclose a cheque for £100. In the hope / that you will be able to do more work for / us, I am sending corrected proof sheets of a documentary / book we are proposing to put out at the end / of the year with the temporary title 'Serve and Preserve', / a survey of all that has so far been done / and can be done to protect the environment. I know / the subject is one that is dear to you. If / you are interested, please telephone me. Yours sincerely, **(178)**

4 THEORY CHECKS

deserve	provincial	achievement	waving
advances	drove	prophesy	definitely
defensive	defects	prophetic	forgive
caves	privately	representative	brave
rift	pavement	chief	cliffs

5 FREE DICTATION

Dear Professor Jones, We hope that in spite of some / delay in gathering all the entries for the essay test, / you are still available to act with the other two / judges in choosing the three best of the one hundred / and ninety-six essays submitted for the prizes of £500, / £250 and £150 / offered. May we ask you to look / again at the rules for judging which we drew up / together? A copy of these is enclosed. The chief points / to be kept in mind are (1) how well the / subject has been covered, (2) the new ideas suggested, (3) / how well the thoughts have been expressed. Our plan is / to send you each a set of copies of the / essays and to ask you to reduce them to ten. / We will then see how closely the results correspond and / meet to decide how to go on from that point. / Yours sincerely, **(162)**

SECTION 14
UNIT 18
of Pitman 2000 First Course

1 SHORT FORM PRACTICE

(*a*)

therefore	more	commercial	to
enlarging	wonderful	enlarge	I
very	there	wonderfully	you
difficult	before	influential	January
thankful	from	his	do
in	anything	that	with
thing	therefore	being	this
wonderful	for	difficult	all
nothing	have	January	thanks
any	be	something	wonderfully

(*b*)

(i) It-is-wonderful to-have such good weather in January. (**10**)

(ii) We-shall-be-there in January and you-may therefore expect to see us. (**14**)

(iii) Thank-you for anything you-can do for-us to-make things less difficult in January. (**16**)

(iv) Before-you-go I-can tell-you you-will-have a wonderful time. (**13**)

(v) This-is a wonderful commercial chance and therefore you-should take-it. (**12**)

2 PHRASES

I have been, I have been there, if there is, I know there is, I will be there, after the, in future, your order, their order, your letter, in your letter, my letter, in my letter, for your letter, I shall be there, you will be there, in their, make their, make their way, in other ways, some other, some other way, my order, for there, for their.

3 DICTATION

(a) Easy

Another matter is that of the supply of typewriters. Who / is responsible for placing the orders is a subject which / we will refer to later, but the main point to / be discussed now is the kind of typewriter to be / ordered. The students must have practice on both pica and / elite machines so we ought to have the same numbers / of both. But it is also essential for both the / teachers and the students that the typewriters should be of / the same make so that it is not difficult to / move from one to another. In future, therefore, we shall / ask for tenders by letter at each of our centres / for a single make of machine from local suppliers. All / the directors at the centres are being asked to meet, / bringing with them their senior teachers of typewriting, to decide / which machines we shall buy. **(145)**

Dear Sir, This afternoon the chief distributor of Icefloe Refrigerators / called on me and asked me to enter into an / agreement with him to take over the remainder of their / stock, for sale in all future orders for this first-/class machine, and to act as a centre for this / particular type. We agreed on terms for this arrangement but / he asked that I should tender for the refrigerators in / writing in the usual way. I wonder if you, knowing / me as you do, will be kind enough to sign / the enclosed form as a witness to my character and / general good standing in this area. Yours faithfully, **(108)**

(b) Standard

I made no fewer than seventeen litres of wine last / year at home and very good it is too. The / secret, of course, is to delay the pleasure of drinking / it as far into the future as you can, since / the wine improves as it matures in the bottle. The / process of fermenting and settling must not be interrupted at / any point or the wine will be ruined. You can / buy products to act as accelerators to the process, but / I do not believe anything is better than the most / natural way. After all, in the great wine-growing centres / of the world they have the wisdom and experience of / centuries to build upon. **(114)**

I am sorry to tell you that the price of / paper is once more to rise by as much as / 24 per cent. The whole problem springs from weaknesses / in the internal structure of the industry. The world demand / for paper rises every year, but the resources from which / paper is manufactured were much abused in the early years, / great forests being felled for paper pulp. The wiser policy / of later years in re-creating forests of fast-growing trees / has not yet matured, though it is hoped that within / a few years paper manufacture will have expanded and prices / will stabilize. (**102**)

(c) Standard

Dear Mr James, In your letter of 24 September, / you asked us to let you know if we were / likely to have eighteenth-century pictures of rural and country / life subjects for sale, and to send you a reminder / in writing of the dates of our autumn sales of / silver. The latter of these is given in the list / enclosed, but you should note those items in Lot 24 / which have been sold by private treaty. I am / pleased to tell you that we shall sell six pictures, / two beautiful studies of horses by Stubbs and four charming / pictures of village life by lesser known artists, but very / accomplished works for all that. Full details are given in / the brochure enclosed. In your case, the present owners, for / whom we act, are prepared to accept private bids before / the day of the sale for two of the less / famous pictures starred in our list. Yours sincerely, (**158**)

Dear Sirs, We carry on business as distributors and factors / for roofing and fencing materials all over the western counties. / Mr Paynter who is, we understand, one of your directors, / has asked us to write officially to you on the / subject of the re-roofing of the Old Manor House just / outside Exeter which you use as a residential centre for / training courses. Such jobs on old historical houses are our / special business. May we therefore arrange an interview with you / for Dennis Winter, our expert in the field? He will / give you detailed advice on your problem, with no charge / of course. Yours faithfully, (**104**)

4 THEORY CHECKS

meter	insulator	counter	tractor
ladder	exporter	scattered	louder
pewter	importer	hinder	signature
orderly	vendor	operator	venture
thermometer	calendar	bother	rendered

5 FREE DICTATION

The history of designing stamps began, of course, with the / most famous of all stamps, the Penny Black of 1840. / Stamp design springs from such needs as engravings for / children's books and transfers on to pottery. These have to / have a simple symbol that is easily understood, and which / has the interest of a picture. They also have to / be capable of being reproduced in a perfect way in / print, thus giving small images of power and simplicity which / are, at the same time, very clear. These are the / things that make a stamp design different from a small / painting. **(101)**

SECTION 15
UNIT 19
of Pitman 2000 First Course

1 SHORT FORM PRACTICE

(*a*)

information	an	will	yesterday
January	therefore	we	thanked
wonderful	thankful	satisfaction	manufactured
enlarge	as	our	unsatisfactory
thanking	but	your	could
wonderful	information	thanking	therefore
enlarge	but	difficult	manufacture
your	will	we	satisfaction
our	could	yesterday	an
unsatisfactory	as	January	thankful

(*b*)

(i) We-hope-that-the manufacture of-these goods is-to your personal satisfaction. **(13)**

(ii) The information we-received yesterday is too-little and unsatisfactory, and-therefore we-cannot act upon-it. **(17)**

(iii) I-thanked him for-the wonderful help he gave us yesterday, but regretted he-could-not join us in January. **(20)**

(iv) We-are thankful that-he did-not enlarge upon-the information we already had. **(14)**

(v) Will-you please express our satisfaction with-the information given, thanking them for-their help? **(15)**

2 PHRASES

large corporation, manufacturing corporation, your attention, immediate attention, prompt attention, our attention, some attention, careful attention, your letter, for your letter, in your letter, their order, your order, if there is, we think there is, I have been, I have been there, in other ways.

3 DICTATION

(a) Easy

Dear Sirs, We have your order for the remainder of / the typewriters and we hope to deliver them to you / later this month. We understand from one of your directors, / Mr Frank Easter, that you have no space to take / them until 28 August. However, we think there is / every chance that we may be able to have them / fully installed and ready for your internal training programme for / operators, due to begin on 4 September. According to our / original tender it was arranged that we would undertake to / fit and test all the machines in the typing stations / and you may rely upon us to carry out this / work as promised. Yours faithfully, **(115)**

Dear Miss Paynter, Thank you for your letter of 14 / September applying for the post of telex operator at our / Message Centre in Manchester. Will you please call for interview / at 3 p.m. in the afternoon of 22 / September at the Message Centre. Mr Smith, one of our / directors, will be pleased to see you at that time / to tell you all about the job before the interview / with Mr Jones. We shall pay all your expenses for / travel, of course, together with a subsistence allowance for the / day of £2. We look forward to seeing you. / Yours sincerely, **(102)**

(b) Standard

The problems of international relations are never solved. Fresh solutions / of the differences between the nations have to be sought / all the time. Television has helped us to realise that / any situation in any part of the world can immediately / affect our own position, and that as one trouble undergoes / examination and decisions are taken to resolve it, another one / will arise in some other section of the globe, and / so on it seems, in endless succession. Only through better / education and the closer co-operation of the great nations in / the United Nations Organization can the dissensions that arise between / man and man be reduced. **(105)**

Your attention is called to a fashion show to take / place on the occasion of the opening of a large / extension to our premises in King Street. We are pleased / to tell you that a wonderful collection from France is / to be modelled for you in celebration of the expansion / of our business which goes on from year to year. / In addition, we have been able to secure those famous / musicians, the Action Makers, to play for you. Champagne and / a selection of cold refreshments will also be provided for / all who attend. We have limited the invitations to those, / like yourself, at the top of the profession. We hope / you will come. Please let us know. **(117)**

(c) Standard

Dear Sir, You asked me for an explanation, if I / had the time, of the market for fiction in this / country and the situation as it might be in a / few years. There is still a large demand for fiction, / but a careful examination of best-sellers reveals that the / subject matter is much more limited than it used to / be. The position is that people look for escapist books / with far away locations and characters, or else go for / the kind of books that have a succession of lively / incidents full of action, of fun, of detail that carries / realism about the writer's research into the background, and characters / larger than life with whom the reader can yet identify. / In the future I expect a transition period and soon / the well-told long story, which has to be written / by authors with a true vocation and a dedication to / their art, will come into its own. Yours truly, **(159)**

Grain growing for human and animal food can be both / a highly profitable and also a highly risky activity. All / kinds of factors have to be taken into account. There / is the weather which can so greatly affect yield. Then / there is the possible loss of crops through insects or / disease. Demand is never steady. Sometimes if a harvest fails / in one area, such as Russia, there is naturally a / raised demand for corn and therefore a better price may / be obtained. Even the decision about the type of grain / to grow is an important one since it has to / be taken largely on intelligent crystal-ball gazing to forecast / the chances for next season. The soya bean may be / the crop to choose perhaps, yet that may be affected / by how great the catches of anchovies are off the / coasts of Peru, since these are a rival in the / cattle feed market. In such a speculative field, some governments / feel it necessary to subsidise their farmers to protect them / against the risks. However, to grant subsidies is in itself / a form of risk. Once farmers begin to rely on / regular subsidies, the improvement of the soil and the application / of the best modern techniques may be neglected. A reduction / in subsidies results in indignant protests from agricultural interests affected. / **(220)**

4 THEORY CHECKS

lighter	indicator	immature	accusation
householder	tractor	natural	transition
importer	duplicator	counter	unnecessary
render	inspector	surrendered	omission
powder	scatter	laughter	elevator

5 FREE DICTATION

It is natural that people should pay attention to fashion, / and try to make their selection of clothes the best / and most modern they can within their means. It should / not be thought that the dedication of women to following / the dictates of fashion is peculiar to them. Men are / in the same situation, only in this age they are / luckier than women because their fashions change more slowly and / less drastically. In the days of the Tudors or of / King Charles II the position was the other way about. / Men had to follow the swift changes in dress and / theirs were the most far-out styles. How the decisions / are taken to change, and how it is that one / idea will be received with jubilation and another die as / soon as born is something we know little about. **(139)**

SECTION 16
UNIT 20
of Pitman 2000 First Course

1 SHORT FORM PRACTICE

(*a*)

knowledge	information	enlarging	particularly
therefore	enlargement	influential	together
enlarger	commercial	difficult	responsibility
wonderful	acknowledge	thankful	subject
January	satisfaction	year	how
information	wonderfully	from	satisfactory
satisfaction	January	before	altogether
knowledge	enlarged	more	responsible
therefore	acknowledge	their	cannot
enlarging	this	very	subject

(*b*)

(i) I-acknowledge with-thanks the information on-the-subject from those responsible. (**12**)

(ii) From-their knowledge of-the very-satisfactory January sales, they-will-be altogether better able-to get more-business. (**19**)

(iii) We-cannot altogether take over his responsibility for-the commercial success of-their venture. (**14**)

(iv) He-is an influential man and-we should therefore get satisfactory information from him. (**14**)

(v) It-is difficult to acknowledge that-he knows more-than we-do but-we should-be very thankful that-we-have him on our side. (**25**)

2 PHRASES

we will inquire, your enquiry, we have enquired, will you inquire, we have several inquiries, our enquiries, we shall require, it will be required, your requirements, their requirements, these requirements, you will require, prompt attention, large corporation, we know there is, for your letter, some other way, in their enquiries, they will be required.

3 DICTATION

(a) Easy

Dear Sirs, In answer to your enquiry, we have to / inform you that we have examined the samples, and they / are better both in quality and in quantity than the / goods supplied. It is quite clear to us that you / have adequate grounds to ask your suppliers to replace two / of the ten bags of wheat with grain of the / right type, and of not less than one hundred pounds / in weight. You will require our detailed answers to your / questions and two copies of these are enclosed. We shall / be glad to act for you if you wish. Yours / truly, (**101**)

The qualifications of this man are quite equal to those / of the first, and he has the advantage that he / speaks the language well and has made frequent trips to / that part of the world. Moreover, he was quick to / answer all our questions on the knowledge of the trade / that is a requirement of the post. We do not / yet know when he could take up the job or / why he has not told us where he was trained. / Our best course now, we suggest, is to make closer / enquiries about the characters of both men before a final / decision is taken. (**103**)

(b) Standard

In looking over the figures you have sent me, I / wonder why our trade in Scotland, where we have always / done so well in the past, is so quiet. All / other regions show a quick increase, especially in the sales / of our new cleaning liquids and household requirements, yet the / Scottish sales show a slight fall. Is this a question / that has some easy answer that I have missed? Is / our new man there equal to the task? We know / he is well qualified and he took over the area / at his own request. I would not wish to make / any hasty judgment. Be inquisitive on my behalf and try / to find out what is wrong. Perhaps our market research / has not been up to its usual high quality. (**129**)

Art is a word that nobody questions and that even / not very well-educated people know and may sometimes use. / But it defies even a linguist to say just what / it means. Whole books have been written about the philosophy / and meaning of art, and whole libraries about its separate / forms. This quotation from an encyclopaedia may help a little: / 'One of man's instincts. In its broadest sense, it is / any form of expression of the spiritual as opposed to / the material aspirations of mankind'. So it always involves imagination / and creation and feeling. Because of its non-material aspect it / is not surprising that it has had, and still has, / links with religion. (**113**)

(c) Standard

Dear Sir, Thank you for your request for a quotation / for building a sun lounge extension to your house in / Quaker Street. An estimate is now enclosed in two parts, / the first for a lounge 23 feet by 12 / feet, and the second for the larger type 30 feet / by 14 feet. As you will see from the details, / not only do we use the highest quality of materials / but we do not cut down in quantities, our policy / being to build a solid lounge for long and trouble-/free use. We can add that nowhere will you get / such a quick and expert job. The excellence of our / workmanship is a subject of frequent praise. Please let us / know within a week whether you will be accepting one / or other of the quotations as we shall need to / requisition the items starred in the estimate which are in / short supply, to be sure of beginning the work on / the date you require it. Yours truly, (**167**)

While the fourth floor is being decorated and re-planned to / take the staff from our Periodicals Department, special arrangements will / have to be made to ensure that the normal work / carries on with as little interruption as possible. The easiest / solution seems to be to take temporary offices for management / staff, thus allowing accounts to go into the offices vacated / for three months. Here we have been lucky in securing / premises next door suitable for the purpose. The move will / take place on Friday next. Intercom has been arranged and / fuller details of the operation are attached. (**97**)

4 THEORY CHECKS

qualify	while	immature	whose
quoted	wheels	inhuman	whistle
bequest	quieter	neither	spread
anywhere	indicator	whenever	quarterly
wharf	immovable	whatever	inadequate

5 FREE DICTATION

If you have not the time for active sport as / a way of getting the exercise that is necessary for / health, then by far the best thing to do is / to walk at least three or four miles each day. / This does not mean a stroll through the streets stopping / now and then to window-shop, but a quick walk / at a pace just a little above what comes naturally / and that induces a gentle perspiration. Try to arrange it / so that you can take a shower immediately after the / walk. The sense of well-being and the fitness you / build up this way will amply repay the effort you / may have to make to walk daily—rain or shine. / **(120)**

SECTION 17
UNIT 21
of Pitman 2000 First Course

1 SHORT FORM PRACTICE

(a)

nevertheless	acknowledge	particular	gentlemen
notwithstanding	enlargement	towards	first
difficulty	subjecting	according to	almost
knowledge	to be	year	several
put	think	larger	largest
influence	nevertheless	ought	dollar
knowledge	also	notwithstanding	had
without	always	largely	difficulty
should	acknowledge	who	on
immediately	owe	large	which
shall	influenced	puts	manufactured
would	notwithstanding	enlarger	has
manufactures	owing	therefore	today
yours	able to	satisfactory	are
nevertheless	trade	difficulty	yourself

(b)

(i) Notwithstanding-the difficulties in-the way we-must nevertheless get-there in-time. (**13**)

(ii) I-have-no knowledge-of what happened; nevertheless I-will-try to help if I-can. (**16**)

(iii) Notwithstanding-the fact that-you have-had these difficulties, it-is nevertheless true that-you still owe-the money. (**19**)

(iv) You ought to-go immediately yourself to see these gentlemen and-try to influence them to acknowledge-their failure. (**19**)

(v) Several of-the largest items have-been manufactured according-to-the method today acknowledged as-the most satisfactory. (**18**)

2 PHRASES

I am confident, we are confident, we shall continue, I will consider, we are considering, in common with the, this committee, in conclusion, in consequence, we shall complete the, we congratulate you, I will inquire, you will require, this arrangement, application form, telephone charges, your attention, large companies, in this business, I hope, this month, sales department.

3 DICTATION

(a) Easy

We shall continue to carry out contracts for countries in / the Middle East this year, and we hope to complete / the building of the dam and the construction of the / oil pipe-line before the end of this calendar year. / The company has very good connections in the area, and / we consider that we are likely to get control of / the pipe-line that is to be laid over a / thousand miles from the main oil fields, to reach the / sea at a point not far south of our existing / installation. We are confident that the success we have had / this year will continue, and that at the end of / this year's business we shall show profits, most of which / it is our aim to reinvest and so enlarge our / business still more. (**133**)

Dear Miss Smith, Can you confirm that the conference of / salesmen which was arranged some months ago to take place / on 14 September in Blackpool, will now take place on / 27 October at the same venue as already arranged? / I have had no official letter, but information has come / to me from our man in that area that this / is the new arrangement. I hope that this is right / as it will be more convenient for me, and in / the circumstances I will not go abroad until the committee / meeting after the conference has been held. Yours sincerely, (**99**)

(b) Standard

Success in business depends upon a number of other factors / as well as ability and knowledge. It is essential to / have a good and steady sense of humour and to / be able to control one's natural feelings and reactions. If / you panic in business, you are lost. In addition, you / must have self-confidence, at least enough to take decisions, / without haste yet promptly, after proper consideration of the factors / concerned in any particular circumstances. It is also necessary to / have the common touch, and to be able to communicate / with, and get on well with, all kinds of people. / It also requires the knack of recognizing opportunity when it / is there, and having the ambition and the compulsion to / 'get on'. All these and other qualities may still not / succeed unless there is also a good share of luck. / (**140**)

Dear Mr Potter, We hope to begin the consumer research / into the five selected washing powders within a week. To / meet your requirements, we have arranged to conclude our work / by comparing the reactions of consumers in the four different / regions selected for the research. As there are over one / hundred separate questions and the chosen consumers in the four / income groups number over three thousand, all results will be / fed into the computer to be analyzed and compared. We / regret the slight delay in the commencement of the project / but we thought it essential to make use of only / experienced and recommended agents, and it has not been easy / to assemble a team whom we were sure we could / rely on. Yours truly, (**124**)

(c) Standard

We have just confirmed the renewal of our office cleaning / contracts for the next calendar year and we have arranged, / as was suggested by the Staff Association, that all carpeting / should be cleaned by vacuum cleaner at least twice a / week. It would be convenient for the contracting company, and / would also make a contribution to reducing our office expenses, / if every office floor were to be kept completely free / of any items except, of course, the furniture of the / rooms. We would ask all members of staff to assist / in ensuring that this is done, and we will consult / with the Staff Association Committee to seek a simple and / practical scheme to effect it. (**115**)

The most famous encyclopaedia in the English-speaking world went / into another edition not long ago. It is the most / complete and comprehensive survey of world knowledge in existence, and / nowadays it has three parts. There is the 'micro' part / which has the amazing figure of 102,000 / entries, each limited to not more than seven hundred / and fifty words. The 'macro' part has only / 4,207 articles but these cover 22,000 / pages and contain twenty-eight million words. The third / part is a volume of eight-hundred pages which is / a systematic outline of all knowledge. Scholars of one hundred / and thirty-one nations have contributed, including over one thousand / from the U.K. (**123**)

4 THEORY CHECKS

recompense	uncommon	consistent	computer
consultant	self-contained	conscious	conversation
consuming	recommend	unconscious	incompetent
recognize	congratulations	completion	inconspicuous
incognito	consist	conductor	encumber

5 FREE DICTATION

Typewriting is probably the office job that occupies most attention / and this is likely to remain so for a considerable / time. The quality and amount of typed matter produced should / therefore be a subject of continuous concern, and so should / the kind of typewriters in use. At the moment it / is probably true to say that neither of these gets / enough attention devoted to it in many offices. We should / always be on the lookout for the best and simplest / ways of tackling every typing assignment, and equally careful to / take advantage of every new step in the design and / facilities offered by new typewriters. Have you a typewriter that / works 10 strokes behind you so that you need never / type a mistake? Or one that will change the line / for you at the right place without your having to / do anything about it? Perhaps you will have one soon. / **(150)**

DICTATION PASSAGES

PASSAGE 1

The press is responsible for creating images and ideas that / the facts,
when you examine them, often do not bear / out. For example, the
press continually presents the picture of / the woman out shopping
for the family provisions, watchful of / every penny, searching round to
50 save two pence on a / pound of tomatoes and counting her change,
checking the items / she has bought, constantly on the alert to spin out /
the housekeeping money to extract the last mite of value / from it. No
doubt there are such women but as / a regular male shopper I can tell
100 you that I / very rarely come across one. Some women never count
the / items they have bought, never keep a check on the / prices that
are being rung up, and never bother even / to look at their change, even
150 when there are pound / notes in it! When I have put this to women /
among my neighbours and friends, none of them tell me / I am wrong.
Instead they say 'Oh, there is just / not enough time' or 'The girl
works so fast I / cannot keep up with her' or 'What I lose on / the
200 swings I expect I shall gain on the roundabouts / anyway'. (**201**)

PASSAGE 2

During the past year we have only just held our / own. In our business,
which is providing holiday facilities both / at home and abroad and
which is very competitive, we / are among the first to feel the effects of
50 rising / prices or of economic difficulties. Those who still go overseas /
take cheaper holidays or go for shorter periods. Many decide / not to go
overseas and take a holiday in this / country, in which case they often
make their own personal / arrangements and do not use the services
that we provide. / Others just cut out a holiday altogether and stay
100 at / home. The net result this year is that we have / had a 32 per cent
fall in our business / and this fact has created many problems, not all
of / which we have been able to solve. We have with / regret had to put
150 off some staff, although we have / done our best by severe economies in
other directions to / minimise this. We have also been obliged to cut
out / some of our package deal holidays altogether, especially those
to / more distant places like the Near East and the African / safari
200 holidays. We have also carried out a policy of / re-locating and reducing
the number of our offices with a / total saving of £513,000. Our / profits
show a reduction of 11 per cent, but compared / with the results of our
competitors we have done well. / (**240**)

PASSAGE 3

I was talking recently with a French gentleman of my / acquaintance.
He is equally at home in both countries and / in both languages and it

was keenly interesting to me / to hear him discourse at large on some of
the / things he had observed about the British and the French. / Among 50
the things he noticed about us was our inborn / friendliness and readiness
to help anyone. The English, he said, / are a nation of eccentrics. Look
anywhere and you will / soon find odd people who do not conform with
the / accepted pattern of life and do the strangest things, like / the 100
people who talk to flowers to make them grow. / He thought we had a
tendency to think that we / are much better than we are, but this was
a / quality we shared with the French who, conceal it as / they may, are
sure that they are the most civilised / race on earth. The French worked 150
hard in order to / live and they were particularly good at shaping life
along / pleasant ways. The British lived to work and when they / were
not working often lacked the knack of enjoying their / life. This, he
thought, was specially true of the Scots / whom he much admired but 200
who he thought usually had / a large chip on their shoulder and only
really relaxed / when the wine and the whisky flowed freely. (228)

PASSAGE 4

Dear Mr Harris, We thank you for your order for / a dozen solid silver
goblets of the type advertised in / last week's issue of The Sunday
Observer. We are writing / now to explain why it is that we are no /
longer able to supply these within one week of the / receipt of order, 50
which was what we stated in our / newspaper notices. These were of
course passed for press more / than eight weeks ago, and since then we
have had / a fire at our works in Edinburgh which has totally / destroyed
most of our plant and all of our offices, / and has also ruined large 100
quantities of our work in / progress. In these circumstances I am sure
you will understand / that we have no hope of getting into full produc-
tion / again for a minimum period of three months. The earliest / date
when we could despatch your order of 20 June, / is 31 October. While 150
we would be very glad / to hold your order and execute it at the earliest /
possible moment, we feel it only right that we should / inform you of
our situation and ask you to decide / whether you wish us to follow this
course or to / return your deposit of £10. We naturally hope that, / 200
understanding our problem and aware of the unique design and / quality
of these goblets, your instruction to us will be / to go ahead with your
order. We enclose a pre-paid / reply envelope and a pro forma to give
you as / little trouble as possible. Yours truly, (256) 250

PASSAGE 5

Most people take some pleasure in reading items like 'What / the Stars Say' and know a little about the signs / of the zodiac, at least their own! Many fewer have / any real belief in the general idea of astrology,

50 that / the time and place of your birth, with the particular / position of
the stars and planets in the sky at / that time, may have a large effect
upon your future / life and fortunes. Nevertheless, the belief in the
influence of / the stars and planets on human character and destiny
100 is / very old. The circle of the heavens was divided into / twelve parts
called 'houses', six above the horizon and six / below it, and these
were supposed to have special influences / on certain aspects of life like
money, marriage, health and / temperament. Also the planets then
known—together with the Sun / and the Moon—also had their particu-
150 lar qualities and influences / as they moved through the houses and as
their positions / changed with relation to one another. This is why
some / words that we use to describe people are derived from / them
like 'mercurial' or 'saturnine'. It is still possible to / find genuine
200 astrologers who are expert in these matters and / will, for a professional
fee, build up the large diagram / which is called a horoscope, which is a
Greek word / that means 'an observation of time'. (**226**)

PASSAGE 6

Dear Sirs, We are shortly moving into large new premises / out of
London, and although we shall of course be / taking with us a con-
siderable part of our office furniture / and appliances, the need to
provide new equipment when we / move means that we shall have a
50 large amount of / material to dispose of at bargain prices. We have
enclosed / a complete list of all these items with details about / the
major ones, the information on which has been supplied / by a reputable
firm of assessors. We would in particular / call your attention to the
100 manual typewriters all of which, / except those in List 3, are less than
ten years / old, have been well maintained and serviced, and are
in / first-class working condition. We also wish to single out / the large
range of office desks of three main kinds / which are available for
150 purchase. We are ready to consider / offers for each or any of these
items provided such / offers are received within twenty-eight days. In
view of / the close relations between our firms over the past four / years,
we are pleased to offer you the first option / on these goods. Should you
200 wish to inspect them, we / shall be glad to receive your representatives
by appointment on / any day after Friday next. Yours faithfully, (**217**)

PASSAGE 7

The technical changes of the past thirty or forty years / have exceeded
in range and number anything that has happened / before in world
history. Moreover, these changes have taken place / with great speed
and at an increasing rate. Not all / have been good, of course, but
50 many have greatly added / to our enjoyment of life. I think in particular

of / the way in which modern electronic and mechanical skill has / enabled us to enjoy music through the long-playing record / and the cassette. Not just to hear it, but to / hear it with such clarity and fidelity of sound as / to be almost totally lifelike. These developments in recent **100**
years / have enabled the manufacturing companies to provide a great range / of recording and playback equipment—and still better—music of / almost endless variety all the way from every form of / pop and 'show-biz' music to the glories of classical / and modern music. No **150**
matter what the mood, I can / find from my growing collection of records and cassettes, the / music to fit it or change it. Like every other / form of art, the more you know about music the / more you can enjoy it. One can only hope that / with so much taped music available more **200**
people will be / encouraged to study music and become players or singers themselves. / **(220)**

PASSAGE 8

In order to cope with the new arrangements of the / departments of our business and the many changes that have / resulted in the actual work that members of staff now / do, it is necessary to produce a new set of / job specifications on which a new and improved salary structure / **50**
may be based. For this purpose the management, advised by / the staff association committee, will produce and distribute within the / next two weeks a revised job specification form to be / filled in by each member of staff. Before asking staff / to complete the form, a blank form with notes on / each section as a guide to writing the job specification, / **100**
will be displayed in each department and in the social / centre, the cafeteria and on all public notice boards. Each / member of staff will be required to fill in his / or her form on his or her own and then / to go **150**
through it individually and confidentially with the department / head. When agreement cannot be reached in this way, the / case is to be referred to the Job Committee composed / of two members of management and two staff association representatives. / It is hoped to implement the new salary structure on / 1st April next. **(203)** **200**

PASSAGE 9

The most fascinating journey I ever took in my life / was by train from the ocean in the west more / than halfway across America to Chicago. It took over three / days during which time we only alighted once from the / train to stretch our legs, yet the time passed all / too quickly. This **50**
was the famous Californian Zephyr, a train / fully equipped with good sleepers, observation cars made mostly of / glass, and excellent facilities for food and drink. We started / out through the great fruit-growing valleys of the Pacific / states and then began to climb up a wonderfully

100 beautiful / river valley, the Feather River, which before long became
a / gorge and then we passed into Colorado and high into / the Rockies
until—even though it was May—we came / to small towns and ski
resorts where snow lay on / the ground. Then we came slowly down off
150 the Rockies / because the descent there was very steep for scores of /
miles, until we suddenly found ourselves on the great plateau / which
was flat but far above sea level, with Denver / glittering in the evening
sunshine 50 miles away. Then through / Salt Lake City, the home of
200 the Mormons, where a / garden has been created out of a desert.
Across the / great open plains of cattle and hog country until at / length
we crossed the mighty Mississippi and reached Chicago, that / huge,
windy and exciting city. (**235**)

PASSAGE 10

The motor-car, which only really arrived on the scene / in this century,
has become a quite indispensable part of / our life. We may complain
bitterly about heavy traffic jams, / the pollution of the air with fumes,
50 and the incessant / noise of the engines. We may look with fear at / the
possible state of our roads in a few decades' / time, when the number of
vehicles has continued to rise / until traffic congestion has brought
movement in the great city / areas to a halt. We may be reminded with
100 sorrow / of the toll of death and injury it exacts. Yet / very few of us
would be prepared to do without / a car having once owned one, and
this is really / not surprising. The car has become the great liberator.
It / takes us places we could not otherwise visit and enjoy, / such as our
150 lovely countryside, and the great houses and / parks it contains. It takes
us to work, it assists / us when we do our shopping, it conveys us to /
cinema or theatre or dance hall, and it is ready / to bear us anywhere on
business or on holiday, all / in far less time than we could do these
200 things / by most other means, and sometimes indeed, is the only / means
by which we could do certain things at all. / So the car will go rolling
on. We only hope / that it will become a quieter, safer and better
controlled / thing. (**241**)

PASSAGE 11

Dear Mr Russell, We have continued to make enquiries about / the
suitcase that you missed when you arrived in Cairo / on the 14th of this
month. We are pleased to / inform you that we now have more positive
information on / the subject. It appears that the airport authorities in
50 Rome / have the case in their possession. In accordance with the /
security arrangements in force there, the case was opened a / few hours
after it remained unclaimed, and when found to / contain nothing but
personal possessions was repacked and held by / the airport police.

Not being able to find any clue / to the identity of the owner, they 100
followed correct procedure / in retaining it while enquiries were made. It seems that / the check-in staff at Heathrow made an unfortunate mistake / in tagging the case with a Rome label instead of / one for
Cairo. Your description of the case with its / identifying mark has now 150
been received and accepted by the / Rome airport police, and BAC have made arrangements / for the case to be delivered to your home within / forty-eight hours. On the matter of compensation we under-
stand / that BAC have written to you already. Yours / sincerely, (201) 200

PASSAGE 12

During my years on earth, now attaining a number I / prefer not to be reminded of, I can recall that / over those decades since the last war I have seen / and heard almost every article of food and drink attacked /
by the medical profession on one ground or another. When / I was a 50
boy, milk, eggs and butter were regarded / as wholesome foods, the real trouble being that people had / not the money to buy enough of them. Now each / of them is suspect. Milk puts on weight, and weight / we
are told is what you must not have. To / be weightless may not be good 100
for a spaceman but / it is good for you. Eggs are a prime source / of that substance that gradually furs up the insides of / our veins and stops our blood from flowing. Butter is / in the same category, and besides, it is
derived from / an animal source, and every item of that kind is / sus- 150
pected of having something to do with high blood pressure / and heart attacks. Bread and cakes are not only made / from flour out of which all the real nutrition has / been extracted, but they are prime weight
builders. Sugar of / any form is hardly better than a deadly poison. 200
Drinking / wine, beer or even water has been assailed by medical / pundits at one time or another. The very air is / full of stuff which will slowly choke your lungs. So / it is becoming dangerous even to breathe.
Perhaps you had / better slip off the planet somewhere while there is 250
still / time! (261)

PASSAGE 13

Please make a note in your diary of the following / dates for the month of September:

(1) On Monday 9 / September, no members of staff should come to work before / 1400 hours. On that day, a bomb from the / 1939
War will be defused and cleared on / the building site at Jacksons, 50
a hundred yards to the / east of our premises, and the police will clear an / area within a quarter-mile radius of the site. It / is expected that this work will be completed not later / than midday, but members
of staff will not be allowed / into the area before 1300 hours. 100

(2) A sherry / party will be held in the reception area on Tuesday /

17 September, and a presentation will be made to Tom / Chivers of
Sales who retires after twenty-nine years' service / with the firm. The
150 Staff Association will also be making / its own presentation, and any
members of staff who wish / to make a contribution will be approached
by Jack Young / or Janet Daly on Friday 13 September.

(3) A general / meeting of the Staff Association to discuss and vote on /
200 three proposals has been arranged for Friday 20 September at / 1630
hours. Please attend if you possibly can. No / proposal can be passed or
minuted as 'not carried' without / the attendance of a quorum of 60
per cent of / members, that is one hundred and sixty voting members
of / the Association.

250 (4) Monday 23 September is the final / day for handing in to the
Accounts Department expenses for / August passed and countersigned
by Heads of Department. (**268**)

PASSAGE 14

Good sound-films in colour, well made for particular educational /
purposes, would seem to be a good and obvious teaching / aid, making
their points in an effective way through the / eye and ear, and backed
up by carefully thought out / teaching scripts. Such films certainly
50 exist in considerable numbers. How / is it then that a recent survey
shows that the / use made of them falls far below what might have / been
expected in secondary and further education? From the results / of the
questionnaire the reasons are clear. First-class projection / facilities are
100 necessary and not many schools or colleges have / these. Then the film
has to be available for showing / at exactly the right time and the right
place in / any course, and very often to arrange this in advance / leads
to many difficulties which teachers are understandably not always /
150 ready to tackle or cannot overcome. Thirdly, the actual showing / of a
film requires expert handling which most places that / have no qualified
technician are unable to provide. The solution / lies in the provision
of a push-button projector which / even the least technically minded
instructor can operate with ease / and the minimum of knowledge. In
200 addition, such a film / showing must be possible in almost any room in
daylight / conditions and with no special preparations being demanded.
Only when / these conditions are fully met, will the colour-sound
film / as an educational and training aid, come into its own. / (**240**)

PASSAGE 15

Dear Miss Strong, Your letter on the subject of refuse / collection from
your house in Aberdeen Road has been passed / to me by the Borough
Engineer, and I will do / my best to answer your questions and help
50 you. I / well understand that, keeping a guest house as you do, / with
as many as ten or twelve guests lodging with / you at a time, you have

much more refuse for / collection than the usual family. If you will be
kind / enough to write on a card the number of plastic / bags you
require for replacement each Monday when the refuse / collection 100
team call, I will arrange with the team foreman / to see that you are
regularly supplied. On the matter / of paper salvage, you will be glad to
hear of / the Council's recent decision that, as from the first day / of
next month, all householders will be asked to separate / clean paper and 150
card waste in a stout transparent bag / to be provided. Paper will be
collected separately at the / same time as the household waste and sold
for re-cycling / to the local paper mills. I regret that for some / weeks
we have been issuing plastic bags of a smaller / size than usual. This 200
has been made necessary because of / a shortage of supplies, and it
seems that we shall / be obliged to continue issuing these smaller bags
for several / months yet before stocks of the larger ones can be / obtained.
I trust that these replies meet all the points / made in your letter. If I 250
can be of any / further help, I am generally available by telephone on
24962. / Yours truly, (276)

PASSAGE 16

Julius Caesar is probably the Roman whose name at least / is known to
almost everyone. He was born in 102 / BC and died by assassination
in / the year 44 BC, when he was fifty-/eight years old. The story of
the famous events that / led up to and followed his death are told by / 50
Shakespeare with great power in the drama that bears that / famous
name. Caesar was first and foremost a soldier. In / his earlier years he
served in Spain, becoming governor of / that province of Rome when
he was forty-one. France, / which was known by the Romans as Gaul, 100
was allotted / to him for a period of ten years, and during / that time
he conquered the whole country up to and / beyond the River Rhine,
and it can be truly said / that he was as great a statesman as he was / a 150
soldier. He brought the civilisation of Rome to France / and established
the centuries of Roman rule, many remains of / which can still be seen
in France to this day. / Twice in this period he invaded Britain, but he
never / stayed long in this country. But he was not without / enemies 200
who envied him his great gifts and power. In / order to overcome
Pompey who was set up as a / rival to him, he was forced to move his
legions / all over Europe and even to Egypt where he had / a love affair
with Cleopatra. He wrote famous books about / his campaigns, and 250
during the height of his power in / Rome, he reformed the calendar
and this has survived to / this day, most of the names of our days and /
months dating from Caesar's time. When his power grew too / great,
and he had in effect become a dictator of / the great Roman Empire, 300
a number of famous Romans united / to kill him and this they did in
the actual / Senate House on the 15th March 44 BC. / (330)

PASSAGE 17

Dear Sirs, We have been informed by our Overseas Sales / Manager,
Mr John Patrick, that you have expressed an interest / in selling your
watches and clocks in South-East Asia. / We are already well acquainted
with the quality of your / products and the value-for-money prices at
50 which you / are able to market them. We have, as I expect / you know,
been general traders in the area for more / than a hundred years,
during which time our name has / become universally known for the
range of goods we deal / in and the excellent and reliable service we
100 provide. We / have a reputation in the East of which we are / proud,
and we should be glad to add the agency / for your manufactures to
our list. We have twenty-six / large stores in all the main cities and
countries of / this large area, our annual turnover running at the
150 moment at / over £4 million sterling. We enclose a map / and a schedule
which show the exact location of each / of our stores, their last year's
trading figures and the / personnel employed. Should your interest
continue, we suggest that a / preliminary meeting be arranged to
200 discuss in general terms the / kind of agency that we could jointly set up.
We / believe that with the growing economic wealth of the region, / the
opportunity for selling timepieces of all types is good. / Will you please
get into touch with us through Mr / Patrick who will be responsible for
250 the initial arrangements? Yours / faithfully, (251)

PASSAGE 18

Your holiday includes, in the price quoted, your flight out / and home
again with a reserved seat on the aircraft / and meals or refreshments
according to the time of day. / Transport from your holiday airport to
your hotel and back / again is provided. Accommodation is always in
50 rooms with private / bath or shower and many also have a balcony.
Three / full meals a day are included with tea or coffee / but not, of
course, drinks. Representatives live in each of / the holiday places
and will be there to meet you / and give you all the help and advice you
100 may / need, including the arrangements for any trips you may wish / to
make while you are there. All charges for hotel / services and taxes are
included, but it is usual to / give tips to waiters or hotel staff who give
150 special / services. The centre pages of our brochure give you up-/to-
the-minute prices for each of our package holidays. / Flight details are
also included giving an easy reference guide / to flights from all the
major cities. These flights are / planned a long way ahead, but there is
usually little / variation in the timings given. You will understand that
200 all / bookings for air holidays are accepted subject to approval of / the
flights by the Civil Aviation Authority. You are strongly / recommended
to take out the special full insurance for your / holiday, details of which
are given on page 10. (239)

PASSAGE 19

Dear Mrs Baker, In connection with the opening of the / Star Hotel
arranged for 13 November next, I am glad / to be able to inform you
that we have been / able to fulfil the whole of your Order No / 0012,
covering the total requirements of one hundred and / twenty sets of 50
cellular blankets, cotton sheets, underlays and pillow / cases with
matching towels, two bath and two hand in / each set. These will be
delivered in one load from / our Newcastle-upon-Tyne works on 28
October. We / are having some difficulties over your second Order
0015. / We have been able to secure all the / brands and sizes you 100
specify of soap, cleaning fluid and / polishes, all of which will be stamped
and embossed with / the Star Hotel logo. The two snags we have run /
into are first, that the impregnated shoe-cleaning papers you / specify 150
are no longer made. We enclose a sample of / an excellent alternative
which could be overprinted as you require, / but I regret to inform you
that this is 25p / dearer for a gross. The second snag is / that although
we can still get rubber bath mats, these / have risen in price by 70 per 200
cent since June. / We suggest as a good replacement the heavy plastic
type, / available in three colours, at 10 per cent lower price / than your
original order. We can recommend it without reserve. / Please let us
know your wishes. Yours truly, (**248**)

PASSAGE 20

This park is one of the loveliest in the country. / It was laid out in the
eighteenth century and many / of the hundreds of trees introduced at
that time from / many foreign countries are now at their best. In
particular, / the willows from China and the great redwoods from
America, / are both very beautiful and impressive. In the centre of / the 50
park, there is a lake running for about two / miles and nearly half a mile
across at its widest / point. In the lake are three islands and two of /
them are crowned by the follies our ancestors were so / fond of building. 100
One is an attractive copy of a / small Greek temple and the other is a
fake ruin / of an old priory. The park also claims to have / the largest
collection of spring flowers in Europe outside of / Holland. In April
there is a large area that is / covered in a great blaze of a million tulips 150
of / all colours, a dazzling and memorable sight. Reached by a / long
uphill path lined with formal beds of flowers and / yew trees, the
mansion stands with its collection of pictures, / silver and gold plate
and magnificent period furniture valued at / over £10 million. (**204**) 200

PASSAGE 21

Dear Mr Lucas, In connection with the enquiries you made / in your
letter to me of 17 February in the / matter of my claim on comprehensive
insurance policy No B4967, / I can give you the following / information:

50 (1) The electric toaster had only recently been serviced / by Times Electrical Limited and I enclose a copy of / their receipted bill. My own electrician, Mr Robert Jenkins of / 12 Main Road, Sunderland, states that there is no doubt / a short circuit occurred, but he is not able to / state definitely whether this was due to the faulty workman-
100 ship / of the service referred to or if it arose from / some accidental cause, such as an artificial contact between the / elements of the toaster.

(2) I enclose an estimate from / R. Broomfield and Sons, builders and decorators, for the repair / and making good of the working surface
150 and side panel / of the dresser that were burned when the accident occurred. /

(3) The two shirts and the slip-on pullover that / my wife had washed and pressed that day, had both / been purchased at Christmas time at Eric Barnes' where I / have an account. I have been able to
200 find the / bill for the purchase dated 23 December and a / copy of this is also enclosed.

(4) As to why / the toaster was left, I would point out again that / there could be nothing unwise or careless about such an / action, since
250 one expects that when the bread has been / properly toasted according to the level selected, it will pop / up and the elements will be shut off. I was / longer upstairs than I had expected, since I had decided / that I needed to shave as well as wash my / hands.

300 May I now hope that in the light of / this information the claim originally made may be settled promptly? / Yours truly, **(312)**

PASSAGE 22

While in Tunisia and crossing a pleasant green plain by / car, I wondered why it was, that in spite of / the hills and the sunshine and the crops, it seemed / a depressing place to me. Then I suddenly realized
50 that / there were no trees. We take the presence of trees / in almost any scene for granted. They are surely one / of the joys of life. There are hundreds of different / species, all with their own quite distinctive shapes, colourings and / foliage. The oldest and largest living things
100 on earth are / trees. Near the Pacific Ocean there are groves of mighty / redwoods, some over three hundred feet high with a diameter / of twelve or thirteen yards and over one thousand years / old. A section of one in the Natural History Museum / in London shows that it was one thousand three hundred / and thirty-five years old before it was
150 cut down. / The wood of different trees is one of the most / useful and beautiful substances available to man, and is worked / in hundreds of ways into objects which range from the / humblest uses to great works of art. But trees in / their natural surroundings are objects of infinite
200 pleasure and interest. / When trees are cut down without some really worthy reason / one cannot help feeling sad. **(215)**

PASSAGE 23

I would point out that, although we deal in a / basic necessity of life in
that we manufacture and sell / clothing, and in this sense we are the
envy of / other manufacturers whose products are more immediately
affected by economic / trends, we have peculiar problems of our own.
In the / first place, because of the stability of our trade, our / profit 50
margins are lower than those in other fields, and / we have to pay
constant attention to our costings and / expenditure in order to achieve
even these low margins. Secondly, / we have to look ahead at least
twelve months in / order to protect ourselves against the market trends 100
that we / foresee. For example, at any time when people have less /
money and feel that their standards of living are threatened, / there is
an immediate move towards off-the-peg suits / and cheaper lines than
the usual English quality clothes. Since / we have no doubt that there 150
will be no great / improvement in the general national situation for at
least two / years, the Board has decided to import on a large / scale
ready-made suits from those countries where, if we / place large orders
for a contract period of more than / a year, we can secure favourable 200
prices. This will enable / us to sell a suit for £35 at / a good profit. (223)

PASSAGE 24

Dear Christopher, I am writing this in the hope that / when you arrive
in Singapore it will be waiting for / you in your hotel. I have very
happy memories of / that place where comfort and service of the highest
order / go hand in hand with glamour and elegance. And what / could 50
be better in the oppressive heat of a tropical / day than to take a swim
in that lovely pool? / However, the point of my letter is not to reminisce /
about hotels but to let you know that your work / in Syria has been
successful, as you said it would, / and the contract has now been signed. 100
That should cheer / you up after the frustrations of India. Two days
after / you arrive in Singapore, we have arranged for Mr Sam / Lee to
call on you. He has a large holding / in the textile business in the area
and I want / you to interest him in our fast weaving machines. Here / is 150
a great chance to establish ourselves in the East / with a product that
none of our competitors can match. / I have every confidence that you
will get us an / order there. As to the extent of it, the enclosed / details of 200
Mr Sam Lee's operations and output in the / area may help you to
decide what to go for. / In order to get this contract and so establish
ourselves / in the East, you may go up to 30 per / cent discount if you
have to. But knowing you, I / expect you will come home with a signature 250
on a / 20 or 25 per cent discounted contract. Don't take / this as an
instruction. It is entirely up to you / to do the best you can. I am sending
Jane / out as far as Rome to meet you on your / way back. Stop off 300

there and take it easy for / two or three days. You will need the break. Yours / sincerely, **(321)**

PASSAGE 25

The principle of one man—one job, does not apply / when it comes to
the letters of our alphabet. The / way we spell very often bears little
relation to the / way the actual sounds that we utter come out. Take /
50 the letter S for example. At the beginning of words / it may have a hard
and sharp hissing sound as / in 'sit'. But in the middle of words or
at / the end it may have a soft, long flat sound / as in 'rose'. Put it in
100 front of a letter / U and it has a third sound as in 'pleasure'. / Put it in
front of the letters I, O, N, / and it has a fourth sound as in 'passion'.
And / then again in some words, nearly all of which come / originally
from French, it is there in the word but / is silent and does no work at
150 all as in / 'island' or 'viscount'. Even this is beaten by the first / letter
of our alphabet, the vowel A which can have / no fewer than eight
different pronunciations. You may find it / interesting to work these
out. To help you, we will / give you three of the least common and leave
200 you / to find the five commoner ones. In the words 'was', / 'village'
and 'many' there is only one A but it / sounds different every time, and
plays the part of other / vowels like O, I and E. **(236)**

PASSAGE 26

Dear Miss Frazer, We have noticed with admiration the excellent /
level of writing and research displayed in your recent article / which
we published last month. It is now our intention / to run a series of
articles, each of about one / thousand to fifteen hundred words, perhaps
50 running to twenty or / more and published either weekly or not less
often than / once a fortnight (to keep the series alive). Our general /
title will be 'Background to Buying' and the idea will / be that we will
take a number of steady consumer / items, as for example, shirts, plastic
100 household goods, frozen foods, / meat, shoes and so on, and write into
the articles / the facts about the market, how the items are made, / the
raw materials, the processes involved and everything of interest / and
significance that the research comes up with. It seemed / to us that you
150 would be the ideal person to / take on such a series. We realise that the
research / will take time, and that you will need help from / a permanent
staff reporter and cameraman. The job therefore, as / we see it, is a
200 full-time one for a / contract period to be decided upon and is worth /
£6,000 a year with expenses. On this provisional basis, / we would
like to know whether the idea interests you. / Yours truly, **(222)**